GIRONA
TRAVEL GUIDE 2024

Discover the Charms of Catalonia

CHARLOTTE BRYAN

Copyright © 2024 CHARLOTTE BRYAN

All rights reserved. No part of this book may be reproduced, stored in a retrieval system, or transmitted in any form or by any means, electronic, mechanical, photocopying, recording, scanning, or otherwise, without the prior written permission of the copyright owner. Always double-check facts, particularly if you're taking a detour to visit a specific location. I fully disclaim any personal or other responsibility, loss, or risk caused by using any of this book's material.

MAP OF GIRONA

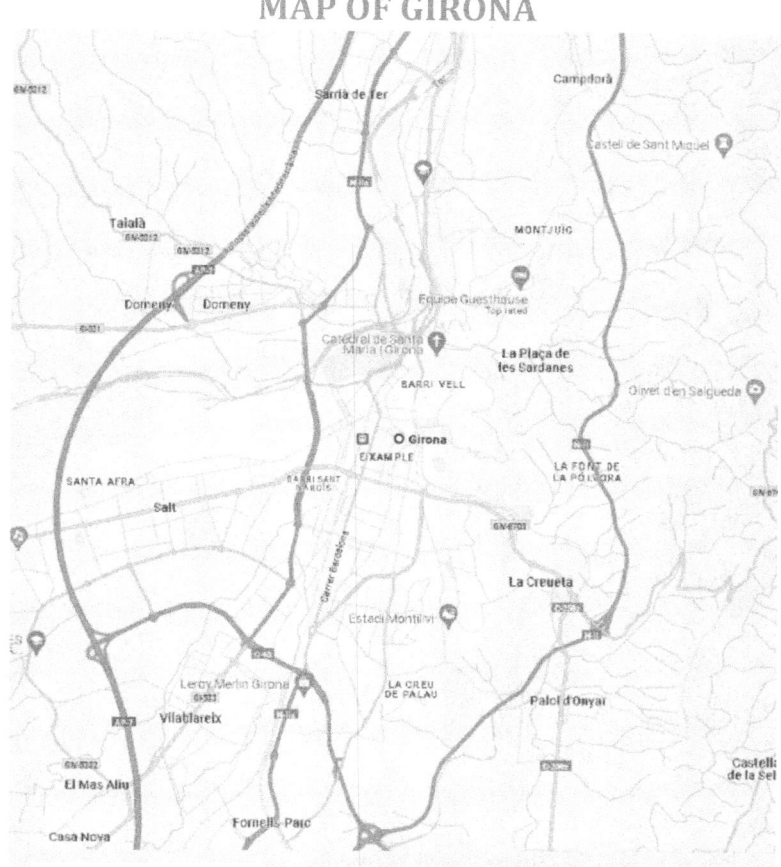

UNLOCK THE MAP OF GIRONA BY SCANNING THE QR CODE TO NAVIGATE YOUR ADVENTURE VISUALLY!

TABLE OF CONTENTS

1. Introduction 8
   - Welcome to Girona 9
   - Why Visit Girona? 11
   - A Brief History 13
2. Planning Your Trip 28
   - Best Time to Visit 29
   - How to Get to Girona 30
   - Packing Essentials 33
3. Getting Around 37
   - Public Transportation 37
   - Biking and Walking 39
   - Renting a Car 42
4. Where to Stay 48
   - Top Hotels in Girona 49
   - Budget Accommodations 55
   - Unique Stays and Boutique Hotels 62

5. Top Attractions 76

    Girona Cathedral 76

    Jewish Quarter (El Call) 80

    Onyar River and Its Colorful Houses 83

    Arab Baths 87

    City Walls (Passeig de la Muralla) 89

6. Museums and Galleries 91

    Museu d'Història dels Jueus 91

    Museu d'Art de Girona 92

    Cinema Museum 94

    Casa Masó 96

7. Exploring the Outdoors 98

    Devesa Park 99

    Hikes and Nature Trails 103

    Cycling Routes 106

    Day Trips to Costa Brava 110

8. Food and Drink 115

    Traditional Catalan Cuisine 115

5

Top Restaurants in Girona 120

Tapas Bars and Cafés 122

Local Markets and Food Festivals 124

9. Shopping in Girona 128

Best Shopping Streets 129

Local Crafts and Souvenirs 134

Markets and Boutiques 137

10. Events and Festivals 142

Temps de Flors 143

Girona Jazz Festival 144

Sant Narcís Festival 147

Cultural Events Throughout the Year 150

11. Nightlife and Entertainment 154

Bars and Pubs 155

Nightclubs and Music Venues 161

12. Day Trips and Excursions 165

Figueres and the Dalí Museum 165

Besalú 168

6

Banyoles and Its Lake 173

Montserrat Mountain 178

13. Practical Information 182

Emergency Contacts 183

Health and Safety 185

Local Customs and Etiquette 188

Basic Catalan Phrases 190

14. Suggested Itineraries 194

One-Day in Girona 195

Three-Day Itinerary 199

Week-Long Exploration 204

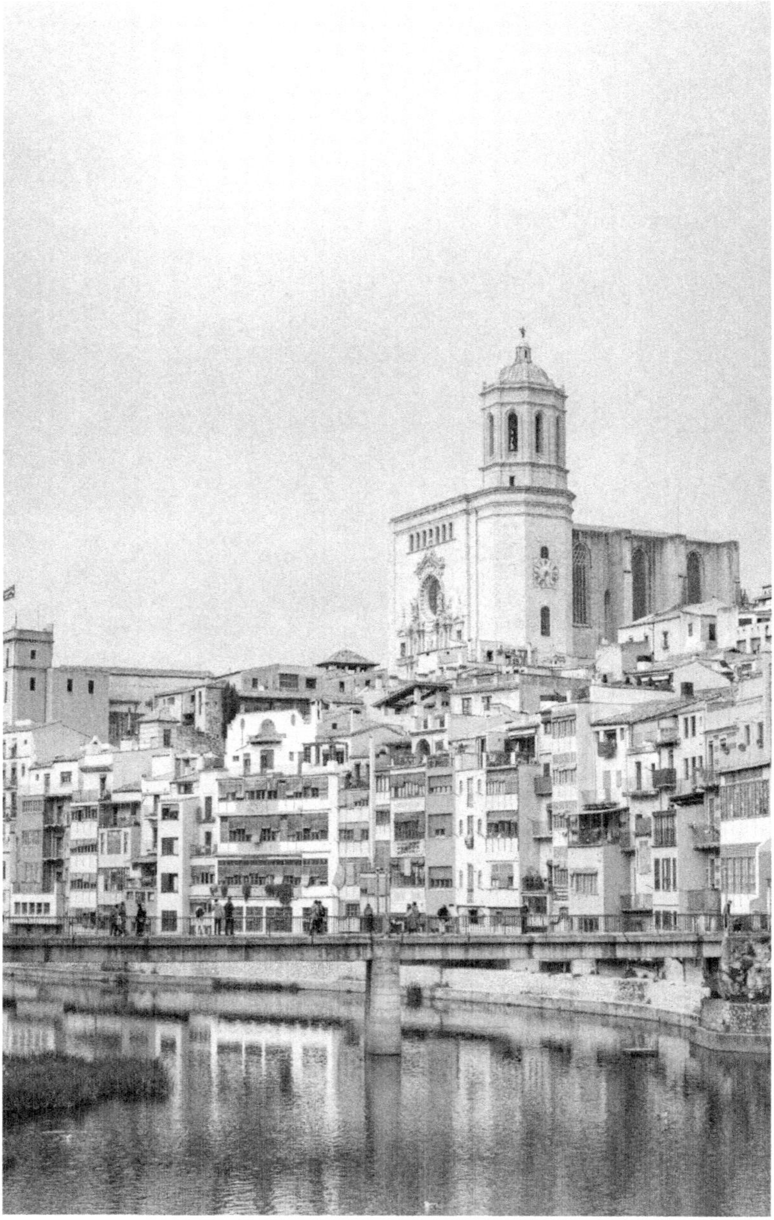

1. Introduction

Welcome to Girona

Ladies and gentlemen, gather around! Oh, what a delight it is to share with you the charm of Girona, a gem nestled in the heart of Catalonia! Imagine stepping into a fairy tale, where every cobblestone whispers stories of yesteryears, and the air is filled with a vibrant mix of history, culture, and pure Catalan spirit.

Picture this: as you stroll through the narrow, winding streets of the old town, you're greeted by the magnificent sight of the Cathedral of Saint Mary, towering above with its grand staircase. It's not just a building; it's a journey back to the 11th century, where every stone tells tales of resilience and grandeur.

Oh, and the rivers! The Onyar River, with its iconic pastel-colored houses lining the banks, creates a picturesque scene that's straight out of a postcard. As you cross the ancient bridges, each step feels like walking through time, connecting you with the medieval essence that Girona holds so dear.

And for all you Game of Thrones fans, you'll be thrilled to find familiar sights, as parts of the city were transformed into the fictional Braavos and King's Landing. Imagine standing where your favorite characters once stood, feeling the magic of both fiction and reality blending seamlessly.

The Jewish Quarter, or El Call, is another marvel. One of the best-preserved in Europe, its labyrinthine alleys and hidden courtyards beckon you to explore and uncover secrets of a bygone era. It's a place where history isn't just remembered; it's lived.

But Girona isn't all about the past. The city pulses with contemporary life, from its bustling markets to its delightful cafes and restaurants, where the flavors of Catalonia come alive on your plate. The people, oh the people! Warm, welcoming, and full of stories, they make you feel at home from the very first smile.

So, come! Lose yourself in the magic of Girona. Let its beauty, its history, and its vibrant spirit enchant you. Trust me, it's a story you'll want to tell over and over again.

Why Visit Girona?

Nestled in the heart of Catalonia, Girona is a city that enchants every traveler with its rich history, vibrant culture, and stunning landscapes. Here's why Girona should be at the top of your travel list:

Girona's history stretches back over two millennia, and its well-preserved architecture offers a window into the past. The city is famed for its impressive medieval walls, which you can walk along for panoramic views of the old town and surrounding countryside. The labyrinthine streets of the Jewish Quarter, known as El Call, are among the best-preserved in Europe, offering a glimpse into the medieval Jewish community that once thrived here.

The Girona Cathedral, with its expansive Gothic nave – the widest in the world – and its Baroque façade, dominates the skyline. The Arab Baths, dating back to the 12th century, provide a serene and historic oasis in the midst of the city. As you explore, you'll find yourself constantly surprised by the beauty of Girona's buildings, from Romanesque to Gothic to Baroque styles.

Fans of the epic series "Game of Thrones" will recognize many parts of Girona, as it was a prominent filming location for the show's sixth season. Walk the same steps as your favorite characters and immerse yourself in the fantasy world that brought the city's ancient streets to a global audience.

Girona's cultural scene is as rich as its history. The city hosts numerous festivals throughout the year, such as the vibrant Temps de Flors, when the streets and monuments are adorned with stunning floral decorations. The city's museums, including the Museum of Jewish History and the Girona Art Museum, offer deep dives into its diverse cultural heritage.

Food lovers will find Girona a paradise of flavors. The city boasts several Michelin-starred restaurants, including the world-renowned El Celler de Can Roca, often ranked among the best in the world. Beyond fine dining, Girona's local cuisine, featuring fresh produce, traditional Catalan dishes, and delectable pastries like xuixo, will delight your taste buds.

Girona is surrounded by beautiful landscapes, from the rolling hills of the countryside to the rugged coastline of the Costa Brava. Outdoor enthusiasts can enjoy hiking, cycling, and exploring the scenic trails that crisscross the region. The River Onyar, which flows through the city, is lined with colorful houses and picturesque bridges, perfect for a leisurely stroll.

The charm of Girona extends beyond its sights and flavors to its people. Locals are noted for their kindness and hospitality, making each tourist feel at home. Whether you're chatting with a shopkeeper in the bustling market or enjoying a coffee in a quaint café, you'll experience the genuine friendliness that characterizes this city.

A Brief History

Did you know that Girona was founded due to a conflict among Romans? And the founding Roman was none other than Pompey the Great. Although he wasn't "Great" yet, he still gets the credit.

Initially, there were the "Indiketes," an indigenous tribe that settled where Girona stands today. The name had various spellings, including Indigetes and Indĭgetæ, but it translates to "indigenous" or "aboriginal." The Indiketes primarily lived near the coast, with their capital, "Indika," located near the medieval Catalan village of Ullastret. Some local historians believe that the site of today's Girona, being further inland, may have also been settled by the neighboring Iberian tribe, the Ausetani, who had their capital in Vic, now part of the comarca of Osona.

Gerunda

The original inhabitants became less significant once the Romans began colonizing the region and the entire Iberian Peninsula. An internal Roman power struggle led to the foundation of Girona. Quintus Sertorius, the Roman Governor of Hispania until 82 BCE, was an enemy of Sulla, the Dictator of Rome. Sertorius formed a coalition with several indigenous Iberian tribes, leading to the Sertorian War, which lasted about eight years.

In 78 BCE, shortly after Sulla's death, the Roman senate sent Gnaeus Pompeius Magnus (later known as Pompey the Great) to Iberia with over 30,000 soldiers to quell

Sertorius' rebellion. One of Pompey's first actions was to build a triangular walled fortress, the initial enclosure of what became the Roman city of Gerunda. This same Pompey later suppressed the Spartacus Rebellion. Parts of the original Roman walls still stand today.

La Força Vella

The fortress, known in Catalan as la Força Vella, remained unchanged until the 9th century when it was expanded and fortified to withstand Moorish invasions, increasing Girona's urban space. Further reconstruction occurred from the late 14th to early 15th centuries. The sandstone walls, averaging 60 meters in height and nearly 2 kilometers in length, are still impressive today.

Despite not being on the coast, Gerunda's location was crucial, as it lay on the Via Heraclea (later the Via Augusta), the only road connecting northeastern Iberia through Narbonne in Gaul to the Italian Peninsula. It was also well connected to the Roman port of Empùries. To experience history, stroll along Carrer de la Força in Girona's Old Town, which traces the old Via Augusta.

The Name

The origin of the name "Gerunda" is uncertain. One theory suggests it derives from "Undarius," the Latin name for the River Onyar, one of the four rivers converging at the city. Another story attributes the city's name to Gério, a three-headed giant said to have founded Girona, but that's a tale for another time!

Christianity

As with the rest of the Iberian Peninsula, Gerunda remained under Roman rule for several centuries. During this time, Christianity gradually spread across Europe, reaching Girona around the early 300s. Although the Romans eventually adopted Christianity as the official religion of their empire, this came too late for Sant Feliu (Saint Felix), who became Girona's first martyr in 307.

Originally from near Carthage in North Africa, Sant Feliu converted to Christianity while studying in Palestine and eventually made his way to Empùries and then Girona. His story has likely been exaggerated over the centuries, but it is said that he was tortured, tied behind horses, and dragged around the town–miraculously healing from his wounds. He was then supposedly thrown into the sea with a mill wheel tied around his neck but saved again by divine intervention. Eventually, he died from having his skin and flesh stripped away with iron hooks.

In 313, just a few years later, Emperor Constantine the Great issued an edict accepting Christianity, and within a decade, it became the official religion of the Roman Empire. After being canonized, Sant Feliu became known as St. Feliu of Girona or St. Feliu the African. Today, many places bear his name, including St. Feliu de Guíxols and St. Feliu de Boada in El Baix Empordà. His tomb is in the Basílica de Sant Feliu de Girona, near Girona Cathedral.

Turbulent Times

Eventually, the 600 years of Roman rule came to an end. The Roman Empire had a tumultuous relationship with the Germanic tribes to the north, and when large numbers of Germanic Goths entered Roman territory fleeing Atila and his Huns, it weakened Rome from within. For Girona, this meant that tribes such as the

17

Vandals, Suebi, and especially the Visigoths began to undermine Roman control of the region. Although many Visigoths converted to Christianity, the Romans still regarded them as barbarians.

As Roman power waned, Iberian territory frequently changed hands. In 395, the Roman Empire split into Eastern and Western Empires. Within less than a century, the Western Roman Empire collapsed and ceased to exist in 480 AD. (The Eastern Roman Empire, with its capital in Constantinople, continued for another millennium, later known as Byzantium.)

Girona came under Visigoth control. The new rulers gradually adopted the language, religion, and much of the culture of their Hispano-Roman subjects, and the practice of applying different laws for Romans and Visigoths was abolished. Although the Visigoth era left little recorded history, they did leave behind some churches. It was during this period that the concept of Hispania as an entity, rather than merely a Roman province, emerged for the first time.

Arab Rule

In the 6th century, Hispania began to see itself as a nascent nation, but things changed again in 711 when the Moors began their conquest of Iberia. By 715, Girona was under Muslim control. The city offered little resistance and thus avoided destruction. Although the Moors built a mosque and confiscated much of the Christian church's property, they did not leave a lasting mark on Girona.

Unlike much of the Iberian Peninsula, Arab control over Girona lasted only 70 years. Located near the edge of Moorish-conquered lands and close to the powerful Kingdom of the Franks to the north, Girona was always vulnerable. The Muslim control in the region was further weakened by infighting among Moorish factions. In 785, some Moorish groups revolted and offered their territories to Charlemagne, King of the Franks, in exchange for military support.

Although the Moors briefly reclaimed Girona, laying siege to it in 793, and sacked it several times, they were eventually driven out. The city then became the seat of the new County of Girona, established by Charlemagne, with Visigoth aristocracy ruling under the Frankish Empire. Many historians consider this County of Girona as the beginning of what would become Catalonia. For 16 years, Girona was the forefront of Carolingian territory against Islam until Barcelona was also captured by the Franks, establishing the Bishopric of Barcelona. Over time, Barcelona surpassed Girona in importance, and in 878, Wilfred the Hairy incorporated the County of Girona into the County of Barcelona.

Nicknames

Medieval Europe had a penchant for colorful monarch nicknames. Apart from Wilfred the Hairy, there were "Charles the Bald," "Charles the Simple," and "Charles the Fat." Charles the Fat's son was "Louis the Stammerer," and another Louis was known as "Louis the Sluggard." Other notable nicknames included "Alfonso the Leprous," "Pippin the Hunchback," "Henry the Impotent," "Raymond the One-Eyed," "Ketil the Flatnose," "Eric the Priest-Hater," "William the Bastard," and "James the Shit." These names reflect the rough-and-tumble nature of medieval kingship, where having a thick skin was essential.

Medieval Girona

Starting in the 10th century, the nobility of the County of Girona and other Catalan counties gradually gained independence from their Frankish overlords, breaking away completely by 987. These territories were effectively ruled by the Count of Barcelona, although not officially recognized as independent. In 1137, a marriage between the Count of Barcelona and the daughter of the King of Aragón led to the formation of the Crown of Aragón.

The medieval period is often regarded as Girona's Golden Age, significantly influenced by its Jewish community. El Call, the Jewish Quarter, functioned almost autonomously, even having its own mayor. The Jewish Kabbalistic school in Girona was a major center of learning in Europe for 600 years. However, persecution increased over time, culminating in a devastating pogrom in 1391 that drastically reduced the Jewish population.

In 1469, the marriage of Queen Isabella of Castile and King Ferdinand of Aragón united their kingdoms, laying the groundwork for modern Spain. Known as the Catholic Monarchs, they were not tolerant of non-Catholics. They established the Spanish Inquisition, expelled the Moors from Granada in 1492, and also expelled the Jews from Spain. Those who remained are forced to revert to Christianity. The same year, Columbus "discovered" the Americas, marking a significant era for the Catholic Monarchs.

Despite the expulsion of Jews, Girona's El Call district is one of Europe's best-preserved Jewish Quarters and a major tourist attraction. The name "El Call" derives from Carrer Major del Call, previously the Via Augusta and now Carrer de la Força. The last synagogue in the city now houses the Jewish History Museum. Overlooking the city are the remains of the Castle of Montjuïc ("Hill of the Jews" in old Catalan), and a former Jewish cemetery was located there.

Girona continued to grow, with extensions and reinforcements of its city walls to protect against numerous attacks. The city faced sieges by French forces in 1653, 1684, 1694, and 1711 as part of larger European conflicts. It was besieged three times by Napoleon in 1808/9, finally falling and remaining under French control until 1813. Plaça de la Independència honors the defenders during these Napoleonic sieges, unrelated to the recent Independentista movement.

The 17th century was particularly tumultuous in Europe, marked by regional wars involving almost every major power. These conflicts, known collectively as the Thirty Years' War, included the Franco-Spanish War and the Catalan Reaper's War. Girona often found itself in the midst of complex conflicts involving the French, Catalans, and Spanish forces.

Spanish Civil War and After

The Industrial Revolution in the 1800s sparked a cultural renaissance in Catalunya, but Girona faced turmoil again during the Spanish Civil War. After the fall of Barcelona to Franco's forces in January 1939, Girona was taken by the nationalists shortly thereafter. Under Franco's rule, the Catalan language was banned, and Girona's name was changed to "Gerona" in Spanish. Police and civil servants from other parts of Spain were brought in to enforce control, censorship was strict, and political freedom was non-existent.

Despite this oppression, Girona grew in the 1950s as migration increased. The city expanded, absorbing surrounding municipalities. Following the end of Franco's regime, streets were renamed in Catalan, the university was founded, and the economy prospered. Girona Province became the wealthiest in Spain, and today, with a population of just over 100,000, Girona is frequently ranked among the best places to live in Spain.

Modern Times

Today, Girona attracts many international tourists annually, thanks to its high-speed train connections to France and beyond and its own Girona-Costa Brava Airport. Visitors often find Girona offers the beauty of Barcelona but in a cleaner, safer, and more manageable setting. The city has also become a global gastronomic hub, with its restaurants winning multiple awards.

Some Legends of Girona

Charlemagne's Chair

Inside Girona Cathedral is an 11th-century throne known as Charlemagne's Chair. Legend has it that if a couple sits together on the throne, they will be married within a year. Conversely, if a man sits alone, he will never marry. Parents who wanted a priest in the family would have their male child sit on the throne. Seminarians were also made to sit on it to keep impure thoughts at bay. Interestingly, Charlemagne never visited Girona; the city was taken by his son, Louis. Charlemagne himself had eighteen children with multiple wives and concubines, making the myth of his chair even more ironic.

The Flies of St. Narcis

In 1285, during a French invasion, soldiers allegedly desecrated the tomb of St. Narcis, Girona's patron saint. Legend says swarms of flies emerged from the tomb and attacked the French troops, killing 20,000 soldiers and 4,000 horses. The French returned in 1653 and 1808, only to be driven out again by the flies. Thus, Girona's symbol became the fly, unique among cities that typically chose more fearsome creatures. It's also said that after St. Narcis's feast on October 29th, flies disappear until the next year.

The Cocollona

This legend involves nuns living near the Onyar River. One devout nun, reproaching the others for their unholy behavior, was locked in the basement. Over the years, she transformed into a crocodile-like creature due to the damp conditions but also grew butterfly wings because of her continued devotion. Known as the Cocollona, she is said to appear swimming in the Onyar on clear full moon nights.

Tolrana's Ghost

Tolrana was a devout Jewish woman murdered one night, her beheaded body found by the city wall near Torre Gironella. Her ghost reportedly roams the streets of the Old Town, singing a sad song.

The Gargoyle of Girona Cathedral

A witch who used to throw stones at the Cathedral and worshippers was turned to stone herself one day. Her petrified form was placed on the Cathedral, making her the only human gargoyle on the structure.

El Tarlà

During a plague outbreak, the street Carrer de l'Argenteria was quarantined. To entertain the bored residents, a local named Tarlà performed acrobatics. After the plague, locals created a puppet in his memory, symbolizing fun and festivities in Girona.

The Lioness' Arse

On Carrer dels Calderes, there's a statue of a lioness, and kissing its backside is believed to ensure a return to Girona or that one might not leave at all. In February 2020, due to the Covid-19 pandemic, the City Council placed a fence around the lioness to prevent kissing and potential virus spread. Although the fence has been removed, the staircase used to kiss the statue has not been reinstated, so this custom is on hold for now.

PLANNING YOUR TRIP

- Best Time to Visit
- How to Get to Girona
- Packing Essentials

2. Planning Your Trip

Best Time to Visit

Girona experiences a subtropical climate with extremely hot summers and cool winters. However, compared to other places in Spain, Girona's weather is relatively mild. Understanding the climate can help you decide the best time to visit. Let's explore the details of each season:

Spring (April to May): During this season, temperatures hover around 22 degrees Celsius. There is some rainfall, making the climate mild and pleasant. Visiting Girona in spring can be advantageous as it is the off-season, leading to fewer crowds at tourist spots.

Summer (June to September): Temperatures can reach up to 30 degrees Celsius, with minimal precipitation. July is typically the driest month. The dry weather makes it easy for travelers to explore the city, making summer the peak season for Girona.

Autumn (October to November): As autumn begins, temperatures cool down. October has the highest rainfall of the year. If visiting during this season, be sure to carry an umbrella or raincoat.

Winter (December to February): Winter temperatures drop to around 13 degrees Celsius, making it quite cool. If you're visiting Girona in winter, pack thick clothing to stay warm.

Rainfall occurs throughout the year, so carrying a raincoat or umbrella is essential. For the best time to visit Girona, late spring and early autumn are ideal, especially for travelers looking to avoid crowds. Alternatively, the summer season is always a popular choice.

How to Get to Girona

Girona Airport

The simplest way to reach Girona is by flying directly into Girona Costa Brava Airport. However, flights are typically available only from within Europe, and during the winter months, they are infrequent. If you manage to secure a flight to this local airport, you'll be just 12.8 km away from the city. While there are no train services from Girona Airport, regular buses run during the day, costing €2.75 for a single ticket.

Barcelona Airport

If a direct flight to Girona isn't available, Barcelona-El Prat Airport is a convenient alternative. Although it's farther away, transferring from El-Prat to Girona is relatively straightforward. Options include:

Sagales Coach: Costs €19.

Taxi Transfer: Approximately €180,

Train: The rapid train takes approximately 40 minutes and costs €17, plus the metro fare from El Prat to Barcelona's main station, Sants. Note that traveling with a bike bag and cases might be challenging on the train.

If arriving at T1, follow signs for the free bus to T2, then proceed to the RENFE station and take the red metro train (R2 line) to Barcelona Sants, a 20-minute ride costing around €4.50. Once at Barcelona Sants, follow signs for the high-speed train (AVE) on platforms 1-6. It's advisable to buy tickets online in advance or use the machines at the station. Keep in mind that the high-speed train may not allow both a large suitcase and a bike box. Alternatively, the regional train to Girona, which takes 1 hour 40 minutes, has no luggage restrictions. Taking a taxi to Barcelona Sants (about €26) and then the high-speed train to Girona is the easiest option.

Madrid Airport

Although Madrid is over 680 km from Girona, it offers more international flight options. You can combine your trip with a visit to the Spanish capital. Direct trains and buses are available from Madrid to Girona.

Train from Other Parts of Europe

For travelers from Europe who aren't in a rush, taking a train might be appealing. Major city stations typically have train services to the area, though you may need to change trains if you have a bike bag and luggage.

Driving from Other Parts of Europe

Driving is a viable option for European visitors. Northern Spain is easily accessible and can be reached relatively quickly from many parts of Europe. Be mindful of tolls, and note that there is ample parking around the city. Look for signs indicating 'gratuit' for free parking.

Packing Essentials

Packing Essentials for Your Trip to Girona, Spain

Girona, a charming city in Catalonia, Spain, offers a delightful blend of history, culture, and scenic beauty. Whether you're exploring the medieval Old Town, savoring delectable Catalan cuisine, or visiting the nearby Costa Brava beaches, packing the right essentials will ensure a comfortable and enjoyable trip.

Here's a comprehensive guide to help you pack for your Girona adventure, considering the weather, activities, and cultural nuances:

Clothing

Weather

Spring (March-May) & Autumn (September-November): Pack comfortable layers such as light sweaters, long-sleeved shirts, and breathable pants. A light rain jacket is also recommended, particularly in spring and autumn.

Summer (June-August): Bring light, comfortable clothing suitable for hot weather. Choose breathable fabrics like cotton and linen in loose-fitting styles. A hat and sunglasses are essential for sun protection.

Winter (December-February): Pack warmer layers like sweaters, a coat, and scarves. While not extremely cold, winter in Girona can be damp and chilly.

Activities

- ❖ For city exploration on foot, comfortable walking shoes are a must.
- ❖ If you plan on hiking or cycling, pack appropriate footwear and sportswear.
- ❖ For evenings out, include a versatile outfit that can be dressed up or down.

Cultural Considerations

Girona is relaxed, but modest dress is appreciated, especially when visiting religious sites.

Women should pack knee-length or longer skirts/shorts and shirts that cover the shoulders. Men should avoid sleeveless shirts in churches and other religious settings.

Essentials

Comfortable Walking Shoes: Essential for exploring Girona's cobblestone streets and charming alleys.

Sunscreen & Hat: Sunscreen is necessary year-round, especially during summer. A hat provides additional sun protection.

Reusable Water Bottle: Important for staying hydrated, especially in warmer weather. A reusable bottle is eco-friendly.

Universal Adapter: If you're traveling from outside Europe, bring a universal adapter. Spain uses a two-pronged plug with round pins.

Small Backpack/Purse: Ideal for carrying essentials like your wallet, phone, camera, water bottle, and sunscreen.

First-Aid Kit: Pack a small kit with basic medications like pain relievers, allergy relief, and bandages.

Quick-Drying Clothes: If you plan any activities involving water, pack quick-drying clothes.

Optional Items

- Swimsuit & Beach Towel: For visits to the nearby Costa Brava beaches.
- Umbrella: Handy during spring and autumn, when rain is more likely.
- Sarong/Scarf: Versatile for use as a beach cover-up, head wrap for sun protection, or light blanket for cooler evenings.
- Spanish Phrasebook: Learning basic Spanish phrases can enhance your experience and interactions with locals.

Additional Tips

- Check Airline Luggage Restrictions: Always check your airline's baggage allowance and restrictions to avoid surprises.
- Pack Light: Girona is walkable, so avoid overpacking.
- Laundry Facilities: Most hotels offer laundry services or have guest laundry facilities.
- Leave Room for Souvenirs: Pack with some extra space in your luggage for souvenirs you may buy during your trip.

3. Getting Around

Public Transportation

By Bus

Local public transport in Girona is operated by TMG (Transports Municipals del Gironès). The city has 12 bus lines, each identified by a different color and numbered from 1 to 12. Buses run daily, including holidays, from approximately 07:00 to 21:30, with slight variations depending on the line. Frequency ranges from every 15 minutes on main routes to every 60 minutes on less busy routes. Buses are ideal for traveling within Girona and to distant neighborhoods. Single ride tickets, known as "Bitllet senzill," cost €1.40 and can be purchased directly on the bus.

On Foot and by Bike

Most attractions and monuments are concentrated in the Old City. For a short visit, staying downtown is recommended as it allows easy exploration on foot. For longer distances, renting a bike is a great option for moving around Girona independently. Various agencies in the city offer bicycle rentals.

ATM Consortium

The Autoritat Territorial de la Mobilitat (ATM) consortium includes a number of operators, including Rodalies de Catalunya. An integrated ticket system allows travel within Girona and 49 neighboring municipalities across eight tariff zones. With a single ticket, you can use all necessary means of transport to move from one point to another.

By Taxi

Taxis are a convenient option for getting around Girona, especially for groups of two or more. Although more expensive than buses, taxis are readily available at the central train station, bus station, city center, Plaça Independència, and Carrer Joan Maragall. Some taxis are equipped to transport disabled people and wheelchairs.

By Car

Using a car in Girona is not recommended, especially in the Old City. If you travel by car, it's best to park outside the Old City and explore on foot.

Biking and Walking

What Does Girona Offer Cyclists?

One of Girona's standout features is its breathtaking scenery, ranging from epic mountain views to the city's beautiful architecture. It is considered one of the best road cycling destinations in Europe, with cycling routes that are renowned worldwide. This reputation has made cycling holidays in Girona increasingly popular.

Girona's status as a premier cycling destination was significantly boosted around 2000 when professional cyclists Lance Armstrong and George Hincapie moved there from Nice, France. Their presence attracted other famous cyclists, transforming the region into a hub for both professional and recreational cyclists. Today, it's common to see pro tour riders at local coffee shops. Girona's appeal extends beyond professionals, attracting cycling enthusiasts of all levels.

What Are the Roads Like?

Girona's roads are quiet, smooth, and well-maintained, offering a variety of cycling experiences. Cyclists generally receive a lot of respect from motorists. The region provides a diverse range of routes, from challenging mountain climbs to easy flat rides to the coast. The city's infrastructure supports cycling with numerous bike shops and local cycling clubs, making it a cycling mecca for all riding styles.

Additional Details

Scenery and Routes: Cyclists can enjoy routes that take them through scenic landscapes, historical sites, and along the beautiful Costa Brava coastline. Notable routes include the Rocacorba climb and the Sant Hilari loop, each offering different levels of challenge and spectacular views.

Local Culture and Cuisine: Girona's vibrant culture and cuisine enhance the cycling experience. After a long ride, cyclists can indulge in local delicacies such as tapas, seafood, and traditional Catalan dishes. Popular spots for cyclists include La Fàbrica Girona and Federal Café, known for their cyclist-friendly atmosphere.

Accommodation and Services: The city caters to cyclists with a range of accommodation options, from bike-friendly hotels to specialized cycling retreats. Services like guided tours, bike rentals, and maintenance support are readily available.

Events and Community: Girona hosts several cycling events throughout the year, including the Sea Otter Europe bike show and various local races. The strong cycling community provides a supportive environment for both new and experienced riders.

Accessibility: Girona's accessibility is a significant advantage. Girona-Costa Brava Airport, located close to the city, offers convenient flights from various European cities, making it easy for international cyclists to visit.

Girona is a cycling paradise offering an unparalleled combination of scenic routes, supportive infrastructure, and vibrant local culture. Whether you're a professional or a recreational cyclist, Girona provides an exceptional experience that is hard to find elsewhere

Renting a Car

Car Rental Policies in Girona, Spain

When renting a car in Girona, Spain, there are a few policies that are unlikely to change over time. Firstly, the legal driving age in Spain is 18 years old, applicable to both residents and tourists. Ensure you carry a valid driver's license and meet the minimum age requirement when renting a car. Secondly, most car rental companies in Girona require a credit card for reservation and payment. This common practice serves as a guarantee for the rental agreement, so it's crucial to have a valid credit card in the main driver's name, as debit cards are usually not accepted. While specific rental policies may vary slightly between companies, these requirements regarding age and credit cards are consistent, helping tourists navigate the car rental process smoothly.

What to Check and Ask Before Renting a Car in Girona, Spain

Before finalizing your car rental reservation in Girona, it's essential to review the rental agreement thoroughly to understand all terms and conditions. Pay close attention to details such as mileage restrictions, fuel policy, and any additional fees. Additionally, check the insurance coverage offered by the rental company to ensure it includes collision damage waiver (CDW), theft protection, and personal liability coverage. Clarifying these aspects beforehand will help avoid surprises during the rental period. Inspect the vehicle for any pre-existing damages and document them with photographs, notifying the rental company of any concerns. Test all essential components of the vehicle, such as brakes, lights, windshield wipers, and air conditioning, to ensure they are in proper working order. By taking these steps, you can have a stress-free experience and enjoy exploring Girona and its surroundings.

Renting a Car in Girona, Spain

Renting a car in Girona is an excellent way to explore the region's stunning landscapes and charming villages. Booking your car in advance is advisable, especially during peak tourist seasons, as Girona's popularity can lead to a scarcity of rental cars. Major car rental companies such as Avis, Hertz, and Europcar operate in

Girona, alongside local agencies like Sol Mar and Goldcar, offering competitive rates. Compare prices and policies to find the best option for your needs, and double-check terms such as mileage limits and fuel policies before confirming your reservation. Collecting your rental car in Girona is straightforward, with major rental companies having desks at Girona-Costa Brava Airport and several offices in the city center. When collecting your car, ensure you have your driving license, passport, and credit card ready. Inspect the vehicle for existing damage and familiarize yourself with its features before driving. With a rented car, you can explore Girona's enchanting wonders at your own pace.

Car Rental Q&A Guide

What documents are required to rent a car in Girona?

You will need a valid driver's license, a passport or ID card, and a credit card for the security deposit.

What Is the Minimum Age to Rent a Car in Girona?

The minimum age to rent a car in Girona is 18 years old.

Do I need an international driver's license to rent a car in Girona?

Typically, an international driver's license is not required if your driver's license is in English or Spanish, but it's best to check with the rental company.

Can I Rent a Car in Girona without a Credit Card?

Most automobile rental firms in Girona demand a credit card for reservations and payments.

Is It Possible to Rent a Car in Girona for One Day Only?

Yes, many rental companies in Girona offer rentals for just one day.

Are There Any Additional Fees or Charges to Be Aware Of When Renting a Car in Girona?

Check for additional fees such as mileage restrictions, fuel policies, and insurance coverage.

What Is the Cancellation Policy for Car Rentals in Girona?

Cancellation policies vary by company, so it's important to review the terms and conditions of your rental agreement.

Is It Possible to Rent a Car in Girona and Drop It Off in Another City?

Yes, many rental companies allow for one-way rentals, but additional fees may apply.

Do Rental Cars in Girona Come with a GPS Navigation System?

Some rental cars come with GPS, but it's best to confirm with the rental company.

What Should I Do in Case of an Accident or Breakdown with the Rental Car in Girona?

Contact the rental company immediately for assistance and follow their instructions.

Why You Should Rent a Car in Girona, Spain

Girona, a stunning city in northeastern Catalonia, offers an enchanting blend of history, culture, and natural beauty. While the city center is best explored on foot, renting a car allows you to discover the surrounding areas at your own pace. With well-maintained roads and excellent connectivity, a rental car provides the freedom to explore the region's hidden gems. Just a short drive away, the Costa Brava offers rugged coastline and idyllic beach towns, perfect for day trips. Additionally, nearby medieval villages like Besalú offer a glimpse into the past with their narrow alleyways and stone bridges. From the charming coastal towns to the picturesque countryside of La Garrotxa, having a car ensures you won't miss any of Girona's captivating sights. So buckle up and get ready for a memorable adventure through Girona and beyond!

WHERE TO STAY

- Top Hotels in Girona
- Budget Accommodations
- Unique Stays and Boutique Hotels

4. Where to Stay

Top Hotels in Girona

Alàbriga Hotel & Home Suites GL

Address: Carretera de Sant Pol, 633, S'Agaro

Price: $625 per night

Facing the beachfront, Alàbriga Hotel & Home Suites GL offers luxurious 5-star accommodations in S'Agaro, featuring a seasonal outdoor swimming pool, shared lounge, and terrace. The property includes a restaurant and bar, along with a hammam for guest enjoyment. The hotel offers 24-hour front desk service, airport transfers, room service, and complimentary WiFi throughout the premises.

Each air-conditioned room at Alàbriga Hotel & Home Suites GL comes equipped with a desk, coffee machine, fridge, dishwasher, safety deposit box, flat-screen TV, balcony, and a private bathroom with a bidet.

Guests can unwind at the spa and wellness center, which includes a fitness center, sauna, and hot tub, or relax in the garden with a children's playground. Nearby points of interest include Cala Maset Beach, Cala Sa Caleta, and Sant Pol. The nearest airport is Girona-Costa Brava Airport, 33 km from the hotel.

Mas de Torrent Hotel

Address: Afores de Torrent, s/n, Torrent

Price: $538 per night

Mas de Torrent, a distinguished member of the Relais & Châteaux brand, stands as the most iconic property in the Empordà region, where every detail exudes exclusivity. The hotel is situated close to the beautiful beaches of Begur, Pals, Tamariu, and Llafranc, and near cultural and historical sites such as Girona's Jewish quarter and the extraordinary Dalí Museum in Figueres, as well as his summer house in Cadaques.

The hotel offers two exceptional dining options. The fine-dining restaurant, considered one of the best in the area, features local seasonal products, while the poolside restaurant offers Mediterranean cuisine in a relaxed atmosphere. Both restaurants benefit from the culinary guidance of Fina Puigdevall, the renowned chef of the two-Michelin-starred restaurant Les Cols d'Olot.

The spa at Mas de Torrent is a sanctuary designed to promote physical and mental well-being, featuring Natura Bisse treatments. The property includes 37 suites, seven of which have private pools, perfectly balancing original architecture with modern design and traditional Empordà rustic style.

This luxurious hotel and spa, featuring both indoor and outdoor swimming pools, is housed in an 18th-century Catalan farmhouse surrounded by lush gardens. Pals is less than a 10-minute drive away. The spa includes a sauna, steam room, and a variety of massage and beauty services. The hotel also offers a fitness center and tennis courts.

All air-conditioned rooms at Mas de Torrent Hotel & Spa, Relais & Châteaux, boast elegant décor with hardwood floors. Some rooms have private pools, while others feature patios with garden views. The restaurant serves gourmet Catalan cuisine with a seasonal menu and extensive wine list, and there is also a bar and terrace.

Guests can enjoy a wide range of outdoor activities in the Baix Empordà region, including hiking, horse riding, and cycling, with free bicycles available at the hotel. There are three golf courses within a 15-minute drive, including Empordà Golf, and the Costa Brava is just a 20-minute drive away.

Hostal de la Gavina GL -

Address: Plaza de la Rosaleda S/N, S'Agaro

Price: £374 per night

Hostal de La Gavina is Catalunya's only five-star Grand Luxe resort hotel, nestled on a small peninsula between two secluded bays, each with a sandy beach, offering an authentic Costa Brava luxury experience. Located just 100 meters from S'Agaro Beach, this 5-star hotel features a spa, tennis club, and outdoor pool surrounded by Mediterranean gardens. The rooms offer stunning sea views.

Situated in an ideal spot on the Costa Brava, Hostal de la Gavina is just 27 km from Girona Airport and 100 km from Barcelona. Figueres, the birthplace of Salvador Dalí, is about an hour's drive away. Hostal Gavina's rooms feature huge windows and classic décor, which includes premium textiles and antique furnishings. All rooms are equipped with air conditioning, a minibar, and satellite TV.

Dining options at the hotel include Candelight by Romain Fornell, a gastronomic restaurant with a bright design that requires prior reservations. The poolside Garbí restaurant serves Mediterranean lunches, and meals and cocktails can be enjoyed on the terrace during the summer.

The Gavina spa has a hammam, hot tub, heated indoor pool, a gym, and a relaxation room with sea views. Guests can choose from a wide range of beauty treatments to enhance their stay.

Suites Natura Mas Tapiolas

Address: Crtra. C-65 Km 7 (Solius), Santa Cristina d'Aro

Price: $375 per night

Suites Natura Mas Tapiolas offers 13 independent suites with private access, each featuring an exclusive garden-solarium. Some suites include an indoor swimming pool with waterfalls, while others are equipped with a double Jacuzzi. Each suite is uniquely named after one of the mountains visible from the property.

Located in Santa Cristina d'Aro, Mas Tapiolas Suites Natura boasts modern, independent suites, each with their own private pool or Jacuzzi®. The property also features a communal outdoor pool, free WiFi, and a terrace. Each air-conditioned suite includes a private garden and state-of-the-art technology, such as a flat-screen TV and Bluetooth speakers. Guests can regulate the temperature and lighting in their suites, and the modern designer bathrooms feature walk-in showers, slippers, and bathrobes.

The hotel's spa offers a variety of amenities, including a salt cabin, ice cave, indoor pool, heated loungers, and a foot bath. A range of treatments is available to guests. Additional facilities include a padel court, fitness center, and an 18-hole Pitch & Putt course.

Guests can enjoy a daily breakfast and dine at the on-site à-la-carte restaurant, which serves meals made from local products. The property also offers a 24-hour reception and free private parking. A variety of beaches are within 10 km, and the Costa Brava Golf Course is just 3 km away. Girona is a 30-minute drive from the hotel.

Budget Accommodations
Hotel Gran Ultonia Girona: A Fantastic Low-Cost 4-Star Hotel

Situated at Gran Via de Jaume I, 22, Hotel Gran Ultonia Girona offers exceptional rooms starting at $80 (excluding taxes). Boasting a range of amenities including room service, a restaurant, a fitness center, a bar, and parking, this hotel provides great value for its guests. With a remarkable guest rating of 8.70 out of 10, it surpasses the average in quality. Located just 0.4 km from the city center, it's an ideal choice for budget travelers. Noteworthy features include laundry services, pet-friendly rooms, a hot tub, and family rooms. After a day of exploration, guests can enjoy the convenience of room service, making their stay even more comfortable. Offering prices below the average for budget hotels, Hotel Gran Ultonia Girona is an excellent choice for travelers seeking affordability without compromising quality.

Hotel Amenities:
- Parking
- Laundry facilities
- Budget-friendly options

Additional Amenities:
- Restaurant
- Fitness center
- Bar/Lounge
- Laundry service
- Pets allowed
- Hot tub
- Family rooms
- Air-conditioned rooms
- Family-friendly accommodations

Hotel Nord 1901 Superior: A Very Affordable 4-Star Hotel

Hotel Nord 1901 Superior offers excellent accommodations starting at $90. This hotel is renowned for its great value, with prices lower than the average for 4-star hotels and guest ratings higher than average, scoring 8.90 out of 10. Located at Nord 7-9 and just 0.3 km from the city center, it provides a relaxing stay with a range of amenities.

Budget Hotel Amenities:

- Outdoor pool
- Parking
- Laundry facilities
- Budget-friendly options

Additional Amenities:

- Restaurant
- Bar/Lounge
- Room service
- Pool bar
- Laundry service
- Bicycle rental
- Child care services
- City views
- Family rooms
- Air-conditioned rooms
- Refrigerator
- Family-friendly accommodations

AC Hotel Palau de Bellavista: A Terrific Budget-Friendly 4-Star Hotel

AC Hotel Palau de Bellavista offers great accommodations starting at $104. Known for its excellent value and family-friendly atmosphere, it boasts a guest rating of 8.30 out of 10. Conveniently located at Pujada Polvorins 1, just 0.6 km from the city center, this hotel provides a comfortable and enjoyable stay with a variety of amenities.

Budget Hotel Amenities:

- Outdoor pool
- Free parking
- Laundry facilities
- Budget-friendly options

Additional Amenities:

- Restaurant
- Fitness center
- Bar/Lounge
- Room service
- Laundry service

- Game room
- Hiking
- Child care services
- Air-conditioned rooms
- Family-friendly accommodations

Peninsular Girona: A Nice Budget-Friendly 3-Star Hotel

Peninsular Girona offers excellent accommodations starting at $78, making it a great value for budget travelers. Located at Avda Sant Francesc, 6, just 0.2 km from the city center, this family-friendly hotel boasts a guest rating of 8.40 out of 10.

Budget Hotel Amenities:
- Parking
- Laundry facilities
- Budget-friendly options

Additional Amenities:
- Restaurant
- Bar/Lounge
- Kid-friendly buffet

- Laundry service
- Bicycle rental
- Car rental
- Kids meals
- Child care services
- Family rooms
- Air-conditioned rooms
- Airport shuttle
- Family-friendly accommodations

Hotel Museu Llegendes de Girona: One of the Best Deals in Girona

Hotel Museu Llegendes de Girona offers fantastic value for a 4-star hotel, with rooms starting at $95. Located at Portal de la Barca 4, just 0.6 km from the city center, it has a stellar guest rating of 8.80 out of 10. This family-friendly hotel provides a comfortable stay with a variety of amenities.

Budget Hotel Amenities:
- Free parking
- Laundry facilities
- Budget-friendly options

Additional Amenities:

- Bar/Lounge
- Room service
- Kid-friendly buffet
- Child care services
- Laundry service
- Bicycle rental
- Car rental
- Family rooms
- Air-conditioned rooms
- Family-friendly accommodations

Hotel Historic: A Fantastic Bargain in Girona

Hotel Historic offers high-quality accommodations starting at $113. Located at C/ Bellmirall, 4A, just 0.4 km from the city center, this hotel has a great guest rating of 8.70 out of 10. It's an excellent choice for families and travelers seeking comfort and convenience.

Budget Hotel Amenities:

- Budget-friendly options

Additional Amenities:

- ❖ Restaurant
- ❖ Rooms with kitchens
- ❖ Hot tub
- ❖ Tour desk
- ❖ Air-conditioned rooms
- ❖ Massage services
- ❖ Balconies
- ❖ Family-friendly accommodations

Unique Stays and Boutique Hotels

1. Can Mascort Eco Hotel

Address:

Can Mascort Eco Hotel

Carrer Raval Inferior 23-25

Palafrugell, 17200 Girona, Spain

Need to Know:

Rooms: 15 total, including two suites.

Check-out: 12 noon, with flexibility based on availability (notify the hotel of your ETA). Earliest check-in is at 2pm.

Prices: Double rooms start at £128.20 (€150), including a 10% tax. Note that there is an additional local city tax of €0.66 per person per night at check-out.

Additional Details: Rates exclude breakfast (available from €20 per person). The hotel offers one room for guests with mobility issues and has an elevator to the first and second floors, which is unique for a historic building.

At the Hotel

Facilities include an apothecary, solarium terrace, herb garden, caldarium, honesty bar, library, bike storage and rental, and free Wi-Fi.

Room amenities include organic cotton towels and bedding, as well as natural and ecological bath supplies. No TVs to ensure a peaceful environment.

Rooms

The rooms feature a minimalist design with white walls, rouged concrete tiles, and wood and wicker furnishings. While simple, each room has unique features such as an original staircase section in Ermedàs or stone arches and beamed ceilings in the Junior Suites. Skylights are included where possible to enhance natural light.

Spa

Relax in the caldarium, a warm, chlorine-free soaking pool under stone vaulted ceilings, followed by sunbathing on the solarium terrace.

Packing Tips

No need for bulky guidebooks; the hotel provides ample literature on local activities. Bring a bike rack for the scenic routes and leave room for the eco-friendly products sold in the apothecary-turned-boutique.

Additional Amenities

The hotel's library offers books on bio-habitability, sustainability, personal development, and healthy eating, as well as board games and a piano. Pets are welcome in all rooms for €25 a night. The hotel provides various room configurations suitable for families but note that there are no TVs.

Sustainability Efforts

The 17th-century building has been carefully updated with bioclimatic design, restored original features, natural materials, solar panels, motion-detecting lighting, and harmonious layout. Plastic use is minimized, toiletries are custom and natural, and breakfast and snacks use local, seasonal products and herbs from the garden. The apothecary store sells eco-friendly goods.

Dining

Breakfast: Served in a charming dining room with terracotta floor tiles and a frescoed ceiling, featuring local and seasonal items like granola with fresh fruit, energy bowls, pastries, and avocado toast with runny eggs.

Snacks: Available from the apothecary, including homemade cake, ice creams, sorbets, cheeses, Empordà-style sandwiches, and pâté. The hotel also offers eco-friendly packed picnics.

Honesty Bar: Open 24 hours with a selection of water, teas, infusions, juices, kombuchas, coffee, snacks, and alcoholic options. Just note down what you consume.

Last Orders

Breakfast: 8:30am to 10:30am

Snacks: 5pm to 9pm

2. Hotel Peralada Wine Spa & Golf

Address:

Hotel Peralada Wine Spa & Golf

Carrer de Rocabertí S/N

Girona, 17491, Spain

Hotel Peralada is dedicated to wine, offering guests the chance to enjoy a variety of wines produced on the historic Peralada Estate. The estate's wines reflect the rich terroirs of Alt Empordà, featuring aromatic notes of pine, rosemary, and eucalyptus. Guests can indulge in vinotherapy treatments at the Wine Spa or dine at the castle's fine-dining restaurant, accompanied by more exceptional wines.

Need to Know

Rooms: 64 total, including 10 suites.

Check-out: Noon. Check-in at 3pm, with flexibility based on availability.

Prices: Double rooms start at £200.70 (€236), including a 10% tax. There is an additional local city tax of €3.30 per person per night at check-in.

Additional Details: Breakfast is available for €35, featuring a buffet and à la carte options in a farmhouse-style room with stone arches, chandeliers, and a terrace overlooking the golf course. The spread includes locally made cheeses, charcuterie, yoghurts, and jams.

Accessibility

The hotel offers two fully accessible rooms and elevators that serve the spa and all floors of the main building.

Hotel Closure

Hotel Peralada is closed from early January to late February.

At the Hotel

Amenities: Golf course, driving range, pro shop, gym, free Wi-Fi, and complimentary house cava on arrival.

Room amenities include a television, a Nespresso coffee maker, a minibar, complimentary bottled water, and Natura Bissé cosmetics.

The Garden Suites feature large terraces with direct access to the hotel gardens and lake, perfumed with the musky scent of jasmine. Each suite is named after operas performed at the annual Festival Perelada, held at the village's castle, such as Carmen, La Traviata, La Bohème, Otello, Turandot, and Andrea Chénier.

Poolside

The saltwater pool in the hotel gardens is open from 9am to 9pm and provides a serene retreat with views of mature olive trees and the Pyrenees.

Spa

The Wine Spa offers a pool, Jacuzzi, and sauna with views of the outdoor pool and surrounding landscape. Guests can book vinotherapy treatments using grape-seed oils, from quick facials to 80-minute full-body massages. A 60-minute session at the Wine Spa water area is available for all guests.

Packing Tips

Bring running shoes for jogging on the country lanes and lakeside paths around the hotel. For golfers, visors are essential to avoid sun glare, though the pro shop offers replacements if needed.

Additional Activities

The hotel features an 18-hole, par 71 golf course spanning 6,070 meters, with a pitch-and-putt, pro shop, and golf school. The driving range provides a picturesque backdrop for those working out on treadmills in the gym.

Dress Code

For a golfer-chic look, opt for pastel colors like lemon, powder blue, and blush pink at the wine bar in the 19th. For evenings in the medieval castle restaurant, go for a more dramatic and elegant style to complement the flickering candelabra.

Hotel Restaurant

Hotel Peralada offers four dining options:

L'Olivera: Featuring local art and a refined Empordà-inspired menu by Michelin-starred chef Paco Pérez, this restaurant serves contemporary Catalonian dishes such as Iberian ham, prawn-stuffed calamari, and cuttlefish with Figueres onion, all paired with Peralada wines.

The 19th: A casual spot for informal bar-style wining and dining.

Garden Bar: Ideal for healthy snacks and an aperitif after a swim.

Castell Peralada Restaurant: Located in the 14th-century Peralada Castle, this fine-dining venue is adorned with chandeliers and candelabra, serving dishes like line-caught hake with saffron clams, Girona veal tenderloin, and honey, olive oil, and orange-blossom ice cream.

Hotel Bar

The Nou Celler 1923 Wine Bar offers an exceptional oenogastronomic experience. Enjoy Girona cheeses and cured meats paired with Peralada wines beneath the stone arches of the former vault, or relax in the evening sunshine overlooking the gardens and vineyards.

Last Orders

The Castell Peralada Restaurant, Celler 1923 Wine Bar, and the 19th are all open until 10pm.

Room Service

Available 24 hours a day, you can order from the room-service menu at any time.

3. Mas de Torrent

Address:

Mas de Torrent
Afueras de Torrent s/n
Torrent, 17123, Spain

Mas de Torrent, a serene getaway from Relais & Chateaux, offers a tranquil retreat with slow pace and charming surroundings. This secluded farmhouse has attracted celebrities like Kylie Minogue, Shakira, and Barbra Streisand. Guests can enjoy various activities, including tennis, biking, yoga, and working out in the gym. For those preferring relaxation, the hotel's Catalan cuisine and signature cocktails by mixologist Manel Vehí are perfect companions.

Need to Know

Rooms: 38 red-tiled rooms, including 34 suites, some with private pools.

Check-out: Noon; earliest check-in at 3pm.

Prices: Double rooms start at £383.29 (€450), including a 10% tax. There is an additional local city tax of €3.30 per person per night at check-out.

Additional Details: Rates include a three-tiered breakfast featuring artisan cheeses, cold meats, and local farm yogurts, with à la carte options such as buckwheat pancakes, avocado and poached eggs, and ham and cheese omelets.

Accessibility

Mas de Torrent is closed during January and February each year.

At the Hotel

Amenities: Free parking, laundry service, WiFi, outdoor pool, indoor lap pool, sauna, hammam, Techno-gym equipment, hydrotherapy pools.

In Rooms: Tea- and coffee-making facilities, hairdryer, Bluetooth speakers, WiFi, bathrobes and slippers, Finca Serena toiletries.

Favorite Rooms

Room seven in the masia is ideal for sun lovers with its large balcony that catches both sunrise and sunset. The garden suites, set away from the main building with private pools, offer extra privacy, making them perfect for honeymooners or those seeking seclusion.

Poolside

Two pools are available: one in the gardens surrounded by palm trees and parasols, and an adults-only lap pool in the spa. Both are open from 7am.

Spa

MasSpa features a hammam, sauna, and Techno-gym equipment, along with 14- and 38-degree hydrotherapy pools. Guests can enjoy Natura Bissé treatments, book a couples room, or indulge in an orange- and lavender-infused massage for added romance.

Packing Tips

Bring comfortable shoes for exploring medieval villages and pedal-able attire for using the free bikes (including e-bikes).

Additional Activities

Space in the spa is reserved for yoga, pilates, and meditation, with mats provided. Private tennis and paddle lessons are also available.

Children

Children's menus are offered at both restaurants, and extra beds and cots can be added to larger rooms.

Dining

Restaurant: Headed by Chef Ramón Freixa, the restaurant serves Catalan cuisine with locally sourced ingredients. Signature dishes include turbot with suquet, baby squid, Iberico chargrilled pork, and an elevated version of the typical Gironan pastry Xuixo.

Hotel Bar: Bar Glicinias offers a sultry ambiance with cocktails by Manel Vehí, such as the 'Sherry Rich' and the 'Green Vibes Detox' mocktail. Many guests start their evenings here before dinner.

Last Orders

Breakfast: 8–11am in the poolside restaurant.

Lunch: 1–3.30pm.

Dinner: Starts at 8pm, with last orders by 10.30pm.

Room Service

Available 24/7, the room service menu includes fresh asparagus salad, Iberian ham, Catalan cheese, braised artichokes, lemon pie, and delicate white wine, ideal for discreet dining.

5. Top Attractions

Girona Cathedral

The Cathedral of Girona is arguably the city's main tourist attraction, drawing millions of visitors annually for its historical significance and appearances in various film and television productions. This ancient building, steeped in history and legends, majestically crowns the city from its highest point in the old town, known as the Old Force, aligned with the urban layout of Gerunda. The cathedral, a monumental structure surrounded by Roman walls and ramparts, showcases architectural styles from different eras, including Romanesque (the cloister and Charlemagne's tower) and Baroque (the facade and grand staircase from the seventeenth century).

Today, notable features from its Romanesque period, dating back to the mid-11th century, include the Gothic nave (the world's widest at 22.98 meters), Charlemagne's tower (Lombard style), the richly sculpted cloister, and the sacristy.

Origins and Evolution

The Cathedral of Girona, known as the church of Santa Maria de Girona, serves as the cathedral seat of the Bishopric of Girona and is the largest Christian temple in the region. Between the fourteenth and eighteenth centuries, the cathedral underwent numerous renovations, starting in 1606 and continuing well into the twentieth century. The bell tower, designed by architect Joan Balcells in 1580, began construction in 1751. The original 11th-century bell tower featured seven stories adorned with Lombard elements such as lesenes, blind arches, sawtooth friezes, and twinned windows with semicircular arches. Its monumental 67-meter-high tower, crowned with a bronze angel, houses six bells, including the notable Benita. Interestingly, the cathedral's clock displays the number four as "IIII" instead of the conventional "IV".

Currently, only the cloister and the northern half of the bell tower remain from the original Romanesque cathedral, with the other half replaced by the Gothic nave. The structure displays a blend of Romanesque,

Gothic, and neoclassical styles. Visitors reach the main door via a large staircase from the late seventeenth century.

Romanesque Cloister and Treasury

The Romanesque cloister of the Cathedral of Girona is renowned for its intricate and rich sculptural details, featuring 122 capitals and decorated friezes depicting historical scenes from the Old and New Testament, human and animal figures, and decorative plant and geometric motifs.

In 2009, the cathedral underwent extensive restoration, including work on the Baroque façade (2001), the bell tower (2003), a museum restructuring project (2006), and the north façade (2009), where a walled window was reopened and a new stained-glass window was installed, designed by Irish artist Sean Scully.

The dilapidated state of Girona Cathedral in 1015 led to the construction of a new Romanesque temple dedicated to Santa Maria, consecrated in 1038. Attached to the church is the Treasury of the Cathedral, which houses three notable pieces of great artistic value:

The Tapestry of the Creation: An almost unique piece globally, possibly crafted in the late 11th century in a local embroiderers' workshop. This 12-square-meter tapestry portrays a medieval vision of the Creation, depicting the origin of heaven and earth.

The Beatus of Girona: A 10th-century copy of the Commentary on the Apocalypse by Beatus of Liébana, featuring more than 100 full-page miniatures.

The Arabic chest of Hixem II: A 10th-century artifact, alongside the Cross of the Enamels from the 14th century.

A Cathedral of Cinema and Series

Girona has gained international recognition, largely due to its well-preserved historical heritage, making it a prime location for filming prestigious television series and films. Girona Cathedral, in particular, has served as a backdrop for notable productions such as the HBO series Game of Thrones and the film The Monk.

Tips for Visiting the Cathedral of Girona in Peace and Quiet

To fully appreciate the Cathedral of Girona, consider hiring tour guides or audio guides. This will enhance your experience, allowing you to explore all the intricate details of the Cathedral, including the Cultural Visit to the Nave, the Treasury, the Cloister, and the Basilica of Sant Feliu. The standard ticket price is approximately €7. Wear comfortable shoes, as exploring the old town of Girona involves climbing many stairs.

One of the best times to visit Girona Cathedral is during Temps de Flors, when the staircases are adorned with stunning floral arrangements, making it the centerpiece of the exhibition. For convenient access, Ultonia Girona Hotels are just a 7-minute walk from the Cathedral and the old town, offering panoramic views of the Cathedral from their terraces.

Jewish Quarter (El Call)

Located within the Força Vella, a mighty Roman fortress built in the 1st century BC, Girona's Jewish Quarter, known as El Call, is one of the city's most iconic areas.

This maze of narrow cobbled streets, stairs, patios, and archways is one of the best-preserved Jewish quarters in the world.

What to See

Museum of Jewish History

Begin your visit at the Museum of Jewish History, housed in an old synagogue. The museum provides an in-depth look at the culture of the Jews in Catalonia and Girona. Highlights include medieval tombstones from the Montjuïc Jewish cemetery in Barcelona and a reconstruction of the famous Rabbi Moshe Ben Nachman.

Tapestry of Creation

The Tapestry of Creation, located in Girona Cathedral, is an 11th-century embroidered tapestry featuring a typical Jewish couple, now symbolic of Girona's Jewish Quarter.

City History Museum

The Museu d'Història de Girona, situated in an old Capuchin convent, offers an excellent overview of the city's history from Roman times. A section of the museum is dedicated to the Jewish history in Girona, where a Jewish community thrived for over six centuries.

Where to Stay

Hotel Historic

Hotel Historic is one of the few hotels located within the old Jewish Quarter. Housed in a 9th-century building, it combines period features with modern comforts. Rooms feature wooden rafters and stone walls alongside contemporary furnishings and designs.

Where to Explore

Carrer de la Força

Carrer de la Força is the main street of the Jewish Quarter. Along this street, you'll find the Jewish History Museum and the City History Museum, ancient doorways, old Jewish houses, and charming boutiques and restaurants. Also, explore Carrer de Sant Llorenç and Carrer Manuel Cundaro, which epitomize the Jewish Quarter with their narrow walls, steep stone steps, and large stone windows.

Where to Eat

Bau Bar

Located next to the imposing Girona Cathedral, Bau Bar is an excellent spot to rest and enjoy a meal while exploring El Call. Besides offering typical Spanish and international dishes, Bau Bar features a special Sephardic menu, allowing you to taste traditional Jewish cuisine.

Onyar River and Its Colorful Houses

One of the city's most captivating features is the Onyar River, flanked by an array of colorful houses that create a stunning, postcard-perfect scene. Here's everything you need to know to fully appreciate and explore this enchanting area.

The Onyar River

The Onyar River is not just a scenic waterway but a lifeline that has shaped Girona's history and development. Flowing gently through the city, it divides the old quarter, Barri Vell, from the newer parts of Girona. The river has been a central element of the city since its foundation by the Romans, who valued its strategic location.

As you stroll along the riverbanks, you'll notice the contrast between the medieval architecture of the old town and the modernity of the newer sections. The river itself provides a serene backdrop, perfect for leisurely walks and reflective moments.

The Colorful Houses

One of the most iconic sights in Girona is the row of vividly painted houses lining the Onyar River. These colorful facades, known as "Les Cases de l'Onyar," create a spectacular visual feast, especially when reflected in the water below. Each house is painted in a different hue, contributing to a vibrant mosaic that changes with the light of the day.

Most of these houses date back to the Middle Ages and have been meticulously preserved. The colors were added in the 20th century, inspired by the cheerful and lively spirit of the Catalan culture. From ochre to bright blue, each color tells a story and adds to the overall charm of Girona.

Girona boasts several bridges that span the Onyar River, each offering unique perspectives of the colorful houses and the cityscape. The most famous of these is the Eiffel Bridge (Pont de Ferro), designed by Gustave Eiffel before he constructed the Eiffel Tower in Paris. The red iron structure provides a striking contrast to the pastel colors of the houses and is a popular spot for photos.

Other notable bridges include the Stone Bridge (Pont de Pedra), which is the oldest and offers a panoramic view of the river and the Cathedral of Girona in the background, and the Gómez Bridge (Pont d'en Gómez), which provides a closer look at the houses' intricate details.

After marveling at the houses and crossing the bridges, venture into the Barri Vell, Girona's old quarter. This area is a labyrinth of narrow, cobblestone streets, ancient buildings, and hidden courtyards. The Cathedral of Girona, with its grand staircase and imposing Gothic architecture, dominates the skyline and is a must-visit.

Wander through the Jewish Quarter (El Call), one of the best-preserved in Europe, where you can explore the

Museum of Jewish History and learn about the rich cultural heritage of Girona's Jewish community. The Arab Baths, another historical gem, offer insight into the city's medieval past.

No visit to Girona would be complete without indulging in its culinary delights. The city's gastronomic scene is renowned, with numerous cafes, tapas bars, and fine dining restaurants. Sample local specialties such as "xuixo," a sweet pastry filled with cream, and savor traditional Catalan dishes at one of the many eateries overlooking the river.

Practical Tips for Visitors

Best Time to Visit: Spring and autumn offer mild weather and fewer crowds. The colors of the houses are particularly striking in the soft light of these seasons.

Walking Tours: Consider joining a guided walking tour to learn more about the history and architecture of the area.

Photography: Early morning or late afternoon light provides the best conditions for capturing the vibrant colors of the houses.

Arab Baths

The Girona Arab Baths (Banys Àrabs de Girona) stand as a Romanesque marvel dating back to the 12th century, commissioned by King Alfons I. Nestled near Girona Cathedral in Girona, Spain, these baths offer a unique and historic experience for tourists.

History of the Girona Arab Baths

The earliest mention of public baths in Girona dates back to 1194. However, the complex suffered partial destruction in 1285 during the siege by the troops of Philip III the Bold of France. Reconstruction efforts took place between 1294 and 1296, and later, in the 17th century, the baths became part of a convent built on the site.

In the 19th century, early travelers documented the baths through drawings and engravings, bringing them to global attention. Subsequently, the baths were purchased, restored, and reopened to the public in 1932.

The Girona Arab Baths Today

Presently, visitors can marvel at the stunning stonework, majestic columns, and rectangular structure of the Girona Arab Baths. The baths feature a frigidarium, apodyterium, and an octagonal pool. Admission prices range from free for children under 8 to 3 euros for full-paying customers.

Occasional concerts are held in the baths, taking advantage of their exceptional acoustics and atmospheric surroundings.

Getting to the Girona Arab Baths

The most convenient way to reach the baths is by bus, disembarking at c. Palamós 1, followed by a 4-minute walk to the site. Alternatively, by car, the journey takes approximately 15 minutes via Carrer Barcelona, while walking through the scenic city center along Carrer de Joan Maragall also takes around 15 minutes.

Notable Mention: Game of Thrones Filming Location

Fans of the popular medieval fantasy series, Game of Thrones, will recognize the Girona Arab Baths from a scene featuring Arya Stark, one of the main protagonists. This connection adds an extra layer of intrigue to the baths, making them a must-visit for enthusiasts of the series.

Today, the Girona Arab Baths continue to attract many visitors, offering a glimpse into centuries of history and architectural brilliance.

City Walls (Passeig de la Muralla)

The origins of the Girona wall trace back to the 1st century BC, coinciding with the Roman foundation of Gerunda. Some studies suggest it might have been built upon remnants of an earlier Iberian wall. Over time, the wall underwent reinforcements during the Roman era to defend against invaders, including barbarian raids.

During the Carolingian era, between the 9th and 10th centuries, significant reforms were undertaken to fortify the wall. Girona's strategic location, positioned between the Carolingian empire and Arab territories, made it a crucial defensive point.

In the 14th century, the medieval wall of Girona emerged. Existing structures, like the Força Vella or old fortress, were fortified, while new walls were erected to protect the growing population in the vicinity. Subsequent reforms and damages from wars shaped the wall's evolution.

Today, these ramparts stand as enduring witnesses to the city's tumultuous history.

What to See When Visiting the Walls of Girona

Passeig de la Muralla Girona (Walk of the Walls of Girona)

This approximately 3 km walk along the walls provides breathtaking panoramic views of the city. From this vantage point, visitors can admire landmarks such as the cathedral, the River Onyar, the Jewish quarter, and the bell tower of San Félix. Walking atop these walls offers a unique perspective and a memorable experience.

6. Museums and Galleries

Museu d'Història dels Jueus

Girona boasts one of the most significant Jewish communities in the Western world, and its Jewish neighborhood, known as the 'call' in Catalan, remains one of Europe's most important. Nestled within this historic enclave is the Jewish History Museum, housed in the Bonastruc ça Porta center. The museum's mission is to illuminate the rich history of Catalonia's Jewish communities.

Museum Overview

The Jewish History Museum features 11 distinct rooms, each offering a captivating journey through the daily lives, culture, and history of medieval Jewish communities in the region, particularly in Girona. Situated in the very space where a synagogue and its ancillary structures once stood in the 15th century, the museum provides an immersive experience into the vibrant past of these communities.

Contact Information

Phone: 972 216 761

Admission

Regular Price: €4

Reduced Price: €2

Free Admission: Every first Sunday of the month

Opening Hours

July and August:

Monday to Saturday: 10am-8pm

Sunday and public holidays: 10am-2pm

September to June:

Tuesday to Saturday: 10am-6pm

Monday, Sunday, and public holidays: 10am-2pm

Museu d'Art de Girona

The Museu d'Art in Girona holds a treasure trove of Catalan art spanning from the 12th to the 20th centuries, making it a cultural gem within the city. Here, visitors can immerse themselves in the rich tapestry of Catalan artistic expression, from religious depictions to legendary tales, all housed within the museum's historic walls.

History and Overview

Originally established to showcase the artistic heritage of Girona and Catalonia, the museum has evolved into a comprehensive collection spanning centuries of artistic evolution. Among its prized possessions is the 10th- to 11th-century altar stone of Sant Pere de Roda, crafted from wood and stone, adorned with religious motifs and Catalan legends. Additionally, the museum serves as a global repository of 20th-century Noucentisme, a Catalan art movement characterized by its rejection of Modernisme in favor of a more classical aesthetic.

Garden Oasis and Unique Perspectives

Beyond its impressive collection, the Museu d'Art offers visitors the opportunity to explore the tranquil Jardins de la Francesa, shaded gardens tucked behind the museum. A staircase within the gardens provides access to the ancient city walls, where visitors can stroll for a considerable distance, gaining a unique perspective on Girona's medieval cityscape.

Opening Hours

July and August: Monday to Saturday: 10am-8pm; Sunday and public holidays: 10am-2pm.

September to June: Tuesday to Saturday: 10am-6pm; Monday, Sunday, and public holidays: 10am-2pm.

Cinema Museum

Located in the heart of Gerona, Spain, the Cinema Museum, also known as the Tomàs Mallol Collection, stands as a testament to the rich history and evolution of cinema. Housed within a building listed in the Inventory of Architectural Heritage of Catalonia, the museum holds both historical and cultural significance.

Museum Overview

The Cinema Museum offers visitors a unique opportunity to delve into the world of cinema and its profound impact on visual culture. Through its permanent exhibition, spanning 400 years of moving image history, visitors can trace the origins and evolution of cinema as both a technique and a visual spectacle. From its humble beginnings to its modern-day iterations, the exhibition provides a comprehensive understanding of cinema's development.

The Tomàs Mallol Collection

At the heart of the museum's permanent exhibition lies the Tomàs Mallol Collection, a vast assortment of cinematographic and pre-cinematographic objects meticulously curated over three decades by Tomàs Mallol himself. This collection offers unparalleled insight into the history and progression of cinema, making it one of the most significant collections of its kind globally.

Practical Information

Address: Carrer de la Sèquia 1, 17001 Girona, Spain.

Phone: +34 972 41 27 77

Casa Masó

Casa Masó, nestled along Carrer Ballesteries, stands as the birthplace of architect Rafael Masó and serves as an emblem of the Noucentisme movement's development in Girona. This architectural gem, seamlessly integrated into the urban fabric, boasts a ground floor, three apartments, and a rooftop terrace.

Originally comprising four artisanal houses acquired by the Masó family, the façade of Casa Masó harmoniously blends Secessionist and Baroque-inspired elements. Along the rear, glass and ceramic colonnades frame breathtaking views of the Onyar river.

Throughout its history, Casa Masó underwent two significant renovations under the guidance of Rafael Masó. The first occurred in 1911 at the behest of his father, aiming to accommodate the needs of a growing and socially prominent family. The second, in 1918, was initiated by his brother upon inheriting the house. These renovations unified the façades, introduced a grand staircase, adorned the interiors with stained glass windows, and crafted bespoke furniture pieces.

In both renovations, Masó embraced the prevailing Modernista style while subtly incorporating elements of the emerging Noucentisme movement. This fusion of styles reflects Masó's innovative approach and his contribution to the architectural landscape of Girona.

Since 2006, Casa Masó has been home to the Rafael Masó Foundation, opening its doors to the public as a cultural institution. Today, it stands as the sole residence along the Onyar river accessible to visitors, inviting exploration into the life and legacy of one of Girona's most celebrated architects.

EXPLORING
THE OUTDOORS

- Devesa Park
- Hikes and Nature Trails
- Cycling Routes
- Day Trips to Costa Brava

7. Exploring the Outdoors

Devesa Park

Discovering Parque de la Devesa

Nestled amidst the historical and cultural riches of Girona, Spain, lies a hidden gem often overlooked by both tourists and locals – the Parque de la Devesa. Spanning over 40 hectares, this expansive park offers a serene escape from urban life, boasting lush greenery, winding paths, and diverse wildlife.

Exploring the Park's Enchanting Beauty

Parque de la Devesa enchants visitors with its picturesque landscapes and tranquil ambiance. From verdant meadows to a serene lake, the park's natural beauty invites exploration and rejuvenation. Wildlife flourishes within its boundaries, with various bird species and fish inhabiting its waters, while a diverse array of plants and trees adds to its allure.

Recreation and Leisure Activities

The park caters to diverse interests, offering a plethora of recreational activities. Visitors can rent bicycles to explore the park's trails, enjoy leisurely strolls along scenic paths, or partake in picnics amidst nature's embrace. Throughout the year, the park hosts a myriad of events, providing entertainment for all ages.

Understanding the Vital Role of Park Biodiversity

Recognizing the importance of biodiversity in parks is paramount for maintaining ecological balance. Parks serve as crucial habitats for numerous plant and animal species, contributing to ecosystem services vital for sustaining life. However, human activities pose threats to park biodiversity, necessitating conservation efforts to safeguard these invaluable ecosystems.

Supporting Park Biodiversity Preservation

Individual actions play a pivotal role in preserving park biodiversity. Engaging in sustainable practices, supporting habitat restoration initiatives, and advocating for conservation measures are effective ways to contribute to biodiversity preservation. By safeguarding park biodiversity, we uphold ecological balance and ensure the well-being of both nature and humanity.

A Guide to Parque de la Devesa

For those seeking respite from urban clamor, Parque de la Devesa offers a tranquil sanctuary. Whether indulging in leisurely walks, enjoying family picnics, or simply basking in nature's serenity, the park provides a rejuvenating escape. With its diverse activities and amenities, Parque de la Devesa beckons visitors to unwind and reconnect with the natural world.

Exploring Outdoor Activities at Parque de la Devesa

Vast Green Spaces for Recreation

Parque de la Devesa beckons outdoor enthusiasts with its expansive green spaces, ideal for a variety of activities. Whether it's a leisurely picnic with loved ones, a spirited game of ball, or an invigorating cycle ride through the park, there's something for everyone to enjoy. For fitness enthusiasts, the park offers a dedicated outdoor fitness area, allowing visitors to exercise amidst nature's splendor.

Nature Walks Among Flora and Fauna

Nature lovers will delight in exploring the diverse flora and fauna that call Parque de la Devesa home. Embark on serene nature walks along the park's trails, soaking in the sights and sounds of the natural world. With several botanical gardens showcasing indigenous plant species, visitors can marvel at the park's botanical diversity while immersing themselves in its tranquil ambiance.

Festivals and Events Celebrating Local Culture

Throughout the year, Parque de la Devesa comes alive with a vibrant array of festivals and events that celebrate the local culture and heritage. From cultural exhibitions to traditional performances, these events offer a unique opportunity to immerse oneself in the rich tapestry of the community's traditions and history.

Amenities for Visitor Comfort

To ensure a comfortable and enjoyable visit, Parque de la Devesa offers a range of amenities. Visitors can avail themselves of restrooms, drinking fountains, and conveniently located picnic areas. Additionally, the park boasts several cafes and restaurants where visitors can refuel and refresh during their outing.

Unveiling the Cultural and Historical Significance

Parque de la Devesa is not just a recreational space; it is also a repository of cultural and historical significance. From hidden landmarks to sacred sites, the park's hidden gems offer a glimpse into the area's rich heritage. By uncovering these treasures, visitors can deepen their appreciation for the park's cultural legacy and historical importance.

Hikes and Nature Trails

The Ultimate Hiking Holiday in the Costa Brava and Girona Pyrenees

Discover a Region of Boundless Beauty and Diversity

Nestled along the Mediterranean coast, the Costa Brava and Girona Pyrenees region beckons travelers with its enchanting blend of natural wonders, rich history, and culinary delights. With over 40 volcanoes, medieval towns, and fishing villages steeped in heritage, this destination offers an unparalleled experience for outdoor enthusiasts and cultural explorers alike.

A Playground for Hikers and Trail Runners

The region's extensive network of trails caters to adventurers of all levels, from casual walkers to adrenaline-seeking trail runners. Whether you're meandering through scenic landscapes or tackling mountain crossings, there's something for everyone to enjoy. The diverse terrain, stretching from the coast to the Pyrenees peaks, provides a captivating backdrop for leisurely strolls, challenging hikes, and exhilarating trail runs.

Iconic Trails and Historic Routes

Embark on iconic trails such as the GR 92 coastal path, tracing the rugged coastline of the Costa Brava. Marvel at breathtaking vistas of beaches, coves, and coastal towns as you journey through stunning natural parks like Cap de Creus and Aiguamolls de l'Empordà. For a deeper immersion into history and wilderness, explore age-old routes like the GR 11 Pyrenean Trail, which traverses majestic mountain ranges and picturesque valleys, offering glimpses of Núria valley and Capçaleres del Ter i del Freser Natural Park along the way.

Cultural Immersion and Culinary Delights

Beyond its natural splendor, the Costa Brava and Girona Pyrenees region boast a rich cultural heritage and a thriving culinary scene. Immerse yourself in the local culture by exploring medieval towns, visiting historic landmarks, and savoring traditional Catalan cuisine infused with avant-garde flair. With 21 Michelin stars gracing its restaurants, the region offers a gastronomic journey that is as delightful as it is unforgettable.

Experience the "Live Twice" Campaign

As part of the "Live Twice" campaign, visitors are invited to discover a destination that is doubly prepared, safe, sustainable, and innovative. Whether you seek wellness retreats, cultural experiences, or outdoor adventures, the Costa Brava and Girona Pyrenees offer an array of activities to satisfy every traveler's desires.

Plan Your Ultimate Hiking Holiday

Embark on a journey of discovery in the Costa Brava and Girona Pyrenees, where breathtaking landscapes, ancient trails, and culinary delights await. Whether you're seeking a leisurely stroll along the coast or a challenging trek through the mountains, this diverse region promises an unforgettable adventure at every turn.

Cycling Routes

Classic Girona Cycling Routes

Girona, Spain, is a paradise for cyclists, offering a diverse range of routes to suit every level of rider. From leisurely countryside loops to challenging coastal climbs, there's something for everyone to enjoy. Here are some classic Girona cycling routes you won't want to miss:

1. Sant Andreu Salou Lanes

Distance: 41 km | Elevation: 281m | Level: Leisure

This quiet loop will take you through peaceful farmland and attractive Catalan villages. Starting from Girona, you'll head south towards Quart and then onto quiet roads through Llambilles and Campllong. Enjoy a coffee stop in Cassa de la Selva before continuing to Sant Andreu Salou and Caldes de Malavella. The route loops back to Girona, offering a perfect warm-up ride for cyclists of all levels.

2. Els Àngels & Santa Pellaia

Distance: 68 km | Elevation: 1,000m | Level: Intermediate

This favorite among pros and leisure cyclists features two gentle climbs surrounded by breathtaking scenery. Starting from Girona, you'll climb Els Àngels, enjoying stunning views before descending into Madremanya and Monells. The route then takes you to Sant Sadurní and the steady climb of Santa Pellaia. Descend into Cassà and Caldes de Malavella before returning to Girona via Sant Andreu Salou and Fornells de la Selva.

3. Costa Brava Classic

Distance: 93 km | Elevation: 1,200m | Level: Advanced

A true Girona classic, this route showcases the stunning Costa Brava coastline and offers a mix of challenging climbs and exhilarating descents. Head south from Girona, passing through Fornells de la Selva and Caldes de Malavella. Climb Sant Grau for spectacular views before descending to Tossa de Mar. After a coastal ride, tackle the climb back to Girona, enjoying familiar roads along the way.

Girona Gravel Cycling Routes

Girona, Spain, is not only a haven for road cyclists but also offers thrilling gravel routes that showcase the region's diverse terrain and picturesque landscapes. Here are some must-ride gravels cycling routes in Girona:

1. Amer Gravel Route

Distance: 52 km | Elevation: 216m | Fitness Level: Intermediate 2/4 | Skill Level: Easy 1/4

Ideal for a leisurely ride on a hot day, this route follows bike paths along the river upstream, passing through the village of Bonmati and reaching Amer. Stop for coffee and food in the historic town square before returning through Àngles and Bescano. With gentle terrain and scenic views, this route is suitable for riders of intermediate fitness levels.

2. Rustik & Dos Kiwis Empordà Classic

Distance: 74 km | Elevation: 227m | Fitness Level: Intermediate 2/4 | Skill Level: Intermediate 2/4

This stunning route features flat terrain and scenic countryside views. Starting from Girona, ride along the banks of the River Ter, passing through forests and farmlands to Rustik, where you can enjoy great coffee and snacks. Continue through picturesque villages and consider a stop at Dos Kiwi's brewery for delicious beers and kombuchas. Return through Stick Farm, enjoying the tranquility of rural landscapes.

3. Rocacorba Dust

Distance: 85 km | Elevation: 1,771 m | Fitness Level: Intermediate 4/4 | Skill Level: Intermediate 4/4

Designed for experienced gravel riders seeking a serious challenge, Rocacorba Dust is not for the faint-hearted. Ride west out of Girona along the Via Verde to Bonmati, then climb over Les Serres into the Vall de Llemena.

Challenge yourself with the ascent to Rocacorba, followed by a thrilling descent through Sant Llorenc and Canet d'Adri back to Girona. Be prepared with supplies as there are limited stops for food and drink along the route.

Experience the Thrill of Gravel Cycling in Girona

Whether you're seeking a leisurely ride or a challenging adventure, Girona's gravel routes offer something for every gravel cyclist. Explore picturesque villages, tranquil countryside, and breathtaking climbs on these unforgettable routes. With options for riders of all skill levels, Girona is the perfect destination for gravel cycling enthusiasts.

Day Trips to Costa Brava

Discover sparkling turquoise waters, picturesque coastal villages, and breathtaking cliffscapes on a day excursion to Costa Brava from Girona. This captivating coastline, located north of Barcelona, offers a refreshing break from the city's rich historical tapestry and immerses visitors in the allure of the Mediterranean Sea. Whether you seek serene beachside relaxation, exploration of charming fishing communities, or a glimpse into authentic Catalan culture, Costa Brava promises an array of experiences. Below is a detailed guide to help you plan your ideal day trip adventure:

Choosing Your Destination

Costa Brava's allure lies in its diverse offerings. Here are some popular options to consider, each providing a distinct experience:

Relaxation on Pristine Beaches: Escape to Platja d'Aro for sun-soaked sands and tranquil swimming spots, ideal for families. Alternatively, explore the secluded coves and hidden bays around Cadaqués, a quaint village renowned for its artistic ambiance.

Exploring Historic Villages: Immerse yourself in the rich heritage and cultural allure of Pals, a medieval town nestled atop a hilltop, offering sweeping vistas of the surrounding landscape. Peratallada, another fortified enclave, boasts well-maintained walls and a labyrinth of narrow alleys waiting to be explored.

Active Adventures: For the adventurous souls, kayak along the rugged coastline of Tamariu, a small coastal hamlet celebrated for its secluded inlets and crystal-clear waters. Alternatively, embark on a scenic hike in Cap de Creus, a natural park showcasing striking rock formations and awe-inspiring sea panoramas.

Planning Your Day Trip

Distance & Transportation: Costa Brava spans over 160 kilometers, so consider travel time from Girona when selecting your destination. Public buses offer convenient connections to most towns and villages. Opting for a rental car provides flexibility and autonomy to explore at your own pace. Trains are also available for destinations closer to Girona.

Organized Tours vs. Independent Travel: Organized tours offer a hassle-free option with transportation, guided commentary, and sometimes meals included. For a more personalized experience, plan your own itinerary using public transport or a rented vehicle.

Time of Year: While Costa Brava welcomes visitors year-round, peak season (July-August) tends to be crowded. Shoulder seasons (April-June & September-October) offer agreeable weather and fewer tourists.

Packing Essentials

Sturdy walking shoes for village exploration or hiking trails.

Swimsuit and beach towel for a refreshing dip in the Mediterranean.

Sunscreen, hat, and sunglasses for sun protection.

Refillable water bottle to stay hydrated throughout the day.

Camera to capture the region's beauty and village charm.

Lightweight jacket or sweater, especially in spring or autumn.

Cash for smaller purchases, as some vendors may not accept credit cards.

Compact backpack to carry essentials while exploring.

Additional Tips

Research Local Festivals: Costa Brava hosts vibrant festivals year-round. Check for any events coinciding with your visit to partake in the local culture.

Sample Local Cuisine: Delight in fresh seafood, paella, and other traditional Catalan delicacies at beachfront eateries or cozy cafes in the villages.

Embrace Siesta: Many shops and establishments close during siesta time (typically 1:30 pm to 5 pm). Plan your activities accordingly or use this downtime to savor a leisurely lunch and relax.

8. Food and Drink

Traditional Catalan Cuisine

Catalan cuisine is a vibrant tapestry of flavors, blending fresh Mediterranean ingredients with centuries-old culinary traditions. From hearty stews to delicate desserts, each dish tells a story of the region's rich cultural heritage.

1. Pa amb tomàquet (Tomato Bread)

Pa amb tomàquet is the epitome of Catalan dining, featuring thick slices of country bread toasted and rubbed with ripe tomatoes, drizzled with olive oil, and sprinkled with sea salt.

Serving Suggestions

Enjoy it for breakfast, lunch, or as a snack, paired with cured meats, roasted vegetables, or Spanish tortilla.

2. Escalivada (Roasted Vegetables)

Escalivada translates to "cooked on hot embers," featuring roasted red peppers, eggplant, and onions, peeled and served cold, drenched in olive oil.

Serving Suggestions

Order as an appetizer alongside pa amb tomàquet for a delightful start to your meal.

3. Esqueixada de bacallà (Shredded Cod Salad)

Esqueixada de bacallà is a traditional salad made with shredded salt cod, tomatoes, black olives, and olive oil.

Serving Suggestions

Enjoy this refreshing salad as a light and flavorful starter.

4. Escudella i carn d'olla (Two-Course Soup)

This hearty two-course soup features a flavorful broth with meat, chickpeas, and vegetables, served with pasta as the first course and meat and chickpeas as the second.

Serving Suggestions

Traditionally served during Christmas, this soup is a comforting and nourishing dish perfect for any occasion.

5. Espinacs amb panses i pinyons (Spinach with Raisins and Pine Nuts)

Spinach is cooked with plump raisins and toasted pine nuts, creating a vibrant dish that balances sweet and savory flavors.

Serving Suggestions

Serve as a side dish or enjoy as a light meal with crusty bread.

6. Calçots amb romesco (Grilled Spring Onions with Romesco Sauce)

Calçots, grilled spring onions, are served with romesco sauce, a chunky blend of roasted red peppers, tomatoes, almonds, and olive oil.

Serving Suggestions

Enjoy this interactive dish with friends, dipping the calçots into the romesco sauce for a burst of flavor.

7. Arròs caldós amb llamàntol (Soupy Rice with Lobster)

This luxurious dish features soupy rice cooked with caramelized onion, tomato sofregit, lobster, seafood, and aromatic herbs.

Serving Suggestions

Indulge in this decadent dish, savoring the rich flavors of the sea and land.

8. Arròs negre amb allioli (Black Rice with Allioli)

Black rice, flavored with cuttlefish ink, is served with allioli, a traditional Catalan garlic sauce.

Serving Suggestions

Pair this flavorful rice dish with allioli for a taste of **Catalonia's culinary heritage.**

9. Canelons de carn (Cannelloni Stuffed with Meat)

Cannelloni pasta is stuffed with braised beef, pork, and chicken, covered with bechamel sauce, and baked until golden and bubbly.

Serving Suggestions

Traditionally served during Christmas, this hearty dish is a festive favorite for families.

10. Suquet de pescadors (Fisherman's Stew with Monkfish and Potatoes)

This simple fish stew features monkfish and potatoes in a flavorful sauce, known as suquet, originating from the fishing villages of the Costa Brava.

Serving Suggestions

Enjoy this comforting stew with crusty bread, savoring the rich flavors of the sea.

11. Mel i mató (Honey with Fresh Cheese)

Fresh cheese is drizzled with honey and garnished with nuts, creating a simple yet satisfying dessert.

Serving Suggestions

Indulge in this sweet treat, celebrating Catalonia's rich dairy tradition.

Top Restaurants in Girona

Must-Try Restaurants

1. El Celler de Can Roca

Iconic Gastronomic Destination: This three-Michelin-starred restaurant has twice been crowned the world's best restaurant in "The World's 50 Best Restaurants." Reservations open on the first day of each month at midnight due to high demand. To secure a table, book well in advance. For a more budget-friendly option, consider dining at "Normal," a restaurant by the Roca brothers.

2. Massana

A Tradition of Excellence: Founded by chef Pere Massana and his wife, Ana Roger, Massana seamlessly blends tradition with innovation. Their signature dish, the Tribute to the duck breast Massana, has been a menu staple since 1986. For a more affordable experience, visit their Nu restaurant, offering modern cuisine in a vibrant setting.

3. Divinum

Haute Cuisine Affordably Priced: Located near Plaza Catalunya, Divinum offers haute cuisine at a reasonable price. Joan Morillo and Laura Tejero curate a gastronomic experience that is both exquisite and accessible. With its spacious and inviting ambiance, Divinum promises a memorable dining experience.

4. Si no fos

Culinary Innovation: Opened in 2019, Si no fos embodies Girona's culinary dynamism. Chef Marc Ramos delivers a "rocky" dining experience with a focus on quality, local ingredients. From premium meats to market-fresh produce, Si no fos offers a culinary journey that delights the senses.

5. Umai

Oriental Delights: For lovers of Japanese cuisine, Umai is a must-visit. Nestled in Plaça Josep Pla, this intimate restaurant boasts impeccable service and top-notch dishes. From muna maki to caramelized foie gras, Umai promises an unforgettable dining experience. Takeaway options are also available for those who prefer dining at home.

Tapas Bars and Cafés

Top Picks for Tapas Bars

Despite its size, Girona boasts a plethora of tapas bars, ranging from traditional to avant-garde. Whether you crave Basque pintxos, Galician seafood, or innovative tapas creations, Girona has it all. Here are some of the best places to indulge in tapas delights:

Txalaka

Basque Flavors: This charming tapas bar offers some of the finest pintxos in the city. Indulge in small slices of bread adorned with Spanish delights like Manchego cheese, mushroom croquettes, cured ham, anchovies, cod, and salmon. With each piece priced at just one or two Euros, you'll find yourself returning to the bar for more.

La Pedra

Croqueta Heaven: Located in the Old Town, La Pedra is renowned for its mouthwatering homemade croquetas.

Savor small fried balls of potato and ham, spinach, or wild mushrooms. Don't miss their delectable patatas bravas served with a spicy tomato sauce and garlic mayonnaise. Pair your tapas with their excellent selection of beers or opt for a filled baguette from their menu.

Tasca Galega Esconxuro

Galician Delights: Experience the flavors of Galicia at this tapas bar, known for its superb seafood bites. Sample traditional dishes like Galician octopus served on a bed of potatoes and sprinkled with paprika, or the delicacy of cod or hake cheeks known as kokotxas.

Zanpanzar

Basque-Inspired Fare: Zanpanzar offers an array of pintxos and shareable tapas plates inspired by Basque cuisine. Delight in dishes like beef cheeks with foie gras or monkfish with broad beans. For heartier options, their lamb and beef stews come highly recommended.

El Vermutet Can Gombau

Vermouth Experience: Embrace the latest trend in Spain with a visit to El Vermutet Can Gombau. Specializing in homemade vermouth paired with tapas, indulge in anchovies, olives, pickled aubergines, and homemade crisps. Visit during 'a la hora del vermut'—vermouth hour—around midday for a delightful aperitif experience.

Local Markets and Food Festivals

Local Markets and Food Festivals in Girona

Girona, a captivating city in Catalonia, Spain, not only boasts a rich history and architectural marvels but also offers a vibrant culinary scene. Delving into the local markets and food festivals provides an immersive experience into Catalan cuisine, featuring fresh seasonal produce, unique delicacies, and the craftsmanship of local artisans.

Local Markets

Mercat del Lleó (Lion Market): Located in the heart of the Old Town, this bustling market is a sensory delight. Open every Tuesday to Saturday morning, it showcases a wide array of fresh, local produce including fruits, vegetables, cheese, cured meats, and flowers. Immerse yourself in the vibrant atmosphere as you explore stalls brimming with seasonal delights.

Weekly Art Fair (Plaça Miquel Santaló): Every Friday afternoon, this charming market exhibits the creations of local artisans. Discover handcrafted jewelry, leather goods, paintings, and other unique souvenirs while supporting the talents of the community.

Artisan Food Products Fair (Rambla Llibertat): Held on the second and fourth Fridays of each month, this fair at Rambla Llibertat offers a haven for local food producers. Sample and purchase artisanal cheeses, cured meats, jams, and other gourmet products, ideal for indulging or creating personalized gift baskets.

Collectors' Fair: Keep an eye out for occasional collectors' fairs throughout the year, where you can unearth treasures ranging from vintage clothing and antiques to stamps and collectibles. Dates and locations vary, so consult the Girona Tourist Office for upcoming events.

Flower Market: Throughout the year, Girona hosts vibrant flower markets, transforming squares into colorful displays. The renowned Temps de Flors (Flower Time) in May highlights floral beauty, while smaller markets add seasonal charm to your visit.

Food Festivals

Temps de Flors (Flower Time): This annual event in mid-May not only showcases flowers but also celebrates culinary delights. Experience a culinary extravaganza with special menus at restaurants featuring floral themes and local ingredients, alongside cooking demonstrations and a festive atmosphere.

Girona Gastronomy Festival: Held in November, this ten-day festival celebrates Girona's culinary heritage. Enjoy delectable dishes crafted by local chefs, participate in cooking demonstrations and workshops, and savor special menus at participating restaurants.

Christmas Market: Experience the festive spirit in December as Girona transforms into a winter wonderland. The Christmas Market offers a delightful selection of local food products, traditional treats, and handcrafted gifts. Warm up with hot chocolate or mulled wine while browsing stalls brimming with holiday cheer.

Additional Tips

Opening Times: Most markets operate in the mornings from 8 am to 2 pm, while food festivals may have extended hours or varying schedules depending on the event.

Embrace the Season: Let the freshest seasonal produce guide your culinary adventures and savor the authentic flavors of Girona.

Sample and Savor: Take advantage of vendor samples to explore new flavors and discover hidden gems within the local culinary scene.

Bring Cash: While some vendors accept cards, it's advisable to carry cash, especially at smaller markets, to ensure seamless transactions.

SHOPPING IN GIRONA

- Best Shopping Streets
- Local Crafts and Souvenirs
- Markets and Boutiques

9. Shopping in Girona

Best Shopping Streets

Shopping in Girona is always a delightful experience, thanks to its vibrant markets and lively streets like La Rambla de la Llibertat and Carrer de la Cort Reial. These areas resemble an open-air gallery where you can leisurely stroll, enjoy a coffee, and shop to your heart's content.

The prime months for shopping in Girona are May, during the flower festival; October, when craft markets fill the streets for the San Narcís festival; and December, when you can find unique holiday products, especially local foods.

Notable Shopping Streets

1. Rambla de la Llibertat

Girona's most significant shopping street, dating back to the 13th century, originally housed a market at the old Pont de Pedra. It's known for its lively shopping atmosphere and distinctive medieval architecture, including colonnades that once sheltered the city's top traders. Named after the Llibertat tree planted in 1869, La Rambla de la Llibertat now features banks, bars, and restaurants, making it a must-visit for both tourists and locals. On Saturday mornings, the street bursts with color and fragrance from its vibrant flower stands. Noteworthy sights include the Modernist façade of Casa Norat and Colmado Moriscot, a picturesque shop selling local spirits and a variety of drinks.

2. Ultònia

Carrer Ultònia is another popular shopping destination, known for its clothing and accessory shops, as well as its charming bars and restaurants, perfect for lunch, dinner, or a traditional vermouth.

3. Calvet i Rubalcaba

This area is home to the famous Mercat del Lleó, a popular market since 1944. Previously, the square outside the city walls hosted farmers and country folk selling their best produce. Today, the indoor market offers a unique place to buy meat, fish, fruits, vegetables, dried fruits, nuts, and spices from Monday to Saturday.

4. Cort Reial

A must-visit cobblestone street in the heart of Girona, especially for tourists, Cort Reial boasts numerous souvenir shops. It's also home to Ulysses, a renowned bookshop specializing in travel books, city and country guides, and mountaineering and nature books. It's the perfect spot for adventurers to find both reading material and travel gear.

5. Argenteria

This pedestrian street extends from La Rambla de la Llibertat and is known for its jewelry, watches, and silver accessories, continuing the tradition of the silver guild that named the street. Unique to Argenteria is the Tarlá, a mechanical acrobat performing tricks on a pole above the street. According to legend, during plague outbreaks between the 14th and 17th centuries, a clown entertained residents who had sealed themselves in their homes. The Tarlá now performs annually on August 27 to commemorate this event.

6. Plaza de Catalunya

This picturesque square span the Onyar River and is a charming spot in Girona, perfect for shopping or enjoying a coffee or aperitif at one of the nearby bars. One of its most unique attractions is the collectors' market held every Sunday from 9 a.m. to 1 p.m. The square fills with stands selling books, postcards, stickers, watches, coins, and even antique furniture, attracting collectors eager to find rare items. Even if you don't intend to buy anything, a visit is worthwhile.

Selected Shopping Centers

1. Centro Comercial Espai Gironès

Espai Gironès is one of Girona's most popular shopping centers, featuring a wide array of famous Spanish and international clothing, footwear, and accessory brands. It's a favorite destination for young people and families. The center also houses supermarkets, a variety of well-known chain restaurants, and a cinema, perfect for rounding out a day of shopping.

2. Comercial Mas Gri

Located on the outskirts of Girona, Comercial Mas Gri offers a handful of large stores and ample parking, making it a convenient alternative to city center shopping. Notable stores include MediaMarkt and Decathlon, catering especially to electronics and sports enthusiasts.

3. Girocentre

Girocentre is essentially the realm of El Corte Inglés. It features a Hipercor and several of El Corte Inglés's prominent departments. Situated on Avinguda de Barcelona, it is close to other El Corte Inglés stores and offers convenient parking.

Where to Stay in Girona

For a relaxing retreat after a day of shopping, consider staying at Hotel Roses Platja. This beachfront colonial-style hotel, located just moments from the center of Roses, offers 167 rooms suitable for couples, friends, or families. Most rooms feature sea views and private terraces, perfect for enjoying sunsets. The hotel boasts a buffet restaurant specializing in healthy Mediterranean cuisine and a snack bar with a terrace ideal for aperitifs or cocktails while taking in spectacular views of the Mediterranean. Additional amenities include gardens leading directly to the beach, a pool with a solarium for peaceful sunbathing, and guest parking (extra charge applicable).

Local Crafts and Souvenirs

Where to Shop for Original Souvenirs in Girona

1. Bussoga

Combine several kilos of Empordà ceramics, Salvador Dalí's surrealism, a good dose of the tramuntana wind, and a handful of skulls, and you get Bussoga. Founded by designer Josep Motas from Sant Jordi Desvalls, Bussoga produces unique ceramic pieces using traditional materials and techniques. It's a perfect blend of tradition, avant-garde, and hipster style, but be warned—it can be addictive.

2. Eva Lozano and Trementina Lab

For exquisite jewelry, visit the workshop of Eva Lozano and Trementina Lab with your phone charged and Instagram ready. Here, you'll find chalk paint art and organic materials alongside elegant earrings and necklaces. Viqui Aldeguer (Trementina Lab) is an interior designer, and Eva Lozano is a jewelry designer. They share a workshop and a philosophy: less is more, with a focus on discretion, subtlety, and organic shapes. All pieces are made in Empordà.

3. Plàstic Store

Sisters Olga and Estrella Roca carry on their parents' legacy of living a rock lifestyle. Their star products are dresses inspired by the '40s, '50s, and '60s, designed to create curves and tiny waists. Their clientele is diverse, from rockabilly fans to women seeking special, flattering outfits. Accessories can transform you into the ultimate Sandra Dee, while the men's section offers mod-style clothing.

4. Vintage

Located just off Plaça de la Independència, Vintage specializes in custom-made shoes crafted using traditional methods. You choose the design, and they make it for you. Expect to wait about a month due to the meticulous process and long waiting list. The price is comparable to eight or ten gin and tonics!

5. Tocat pel vent

"Touched by the wind" expresses a deep love for Empordà and its winds. This shop, which doubles as an interior design and creative lighting studio, sells locally made items like La Bisbal ceramics and works by Empordà artists. They also create unique lamps and restore old furniture in their Camallera workshop.

6. Nausica Masó Orfebre

Jewelry designer Nausica Masó, granddaughter of renowned Girona architect Rafael Masó, draws inspiration from the modernista movement. Her pieces, made from new or recycled precious metals, blend organic and rational elements. Her creations range from geometric designs with architectural influences to ethnic styles and works inspired directly by her famous grandfather.

7. Portal del Col·leccionista

Despite Girona's bourgeois and historic pride, it has few old bookshops or antique dealers. El Portal del Col·leccionista is a noteworthy exception. This small family business in the Jewish quarter has been open for 40 years and offers items ranging from 1920s gossip magazines to rare objects coveted by bibliophiles. Don't be deterred by the crowded space—take your time browsing through old postcards, cinema posters, soda siphons, stickers, and rare editions.

Markets and Boutiques

Girona, a captivating city in Catalonia, Spain, offers a treasure trove for shopaholics and souvenir hunters alike. Beyond the renowned historical sites, Girona boasts a vibrant shopping scene, where bustling markets overflow with local produce and handcrafted goods, while charming boutiques showcase unique finds and designer labels.

Market Escapades

Lion's Roar Market (Mercat del Lleó): Nestled in the heart of the Old Town, this bustling market is a must-visit for foodies and those seeking a taste of local life. Open Tuesdays to Saturdays, it offers a maze of stalls brimming with fresh, seasonal produce – fruits, vegetables, cheese, cured meats, and even flowers. Immerse yourself in the vibrant ambiance as you explore the freshest offerings of the region.

Artisan Crafts Fair (Plaça Miquel Santaló): Held every Friday afternoon, this charming market showcases the craftsmanship of local artisans. Discover handcrafted jewelry, leather goods, paintings, and other unique souvenirs, all while supporting the thriving local artist community.

Gourmet Finds Fair (Rambla Llibertat): Venture to Rambla Llibertat on the second and fourth Fridays of each month to indulge in a haven for local food producers. Sample and purchase artisanal cheeses, cured meats, delicious jams, and other gourmet delights, perfect for savoring or creating bespoke gift baskets.

Treasure Trove Collectors' Fair: Delve into occasional collectors' fairs held throughout the year, where you can unearth vintage clothing, antiques, stamps, and collectibles. Dates and locations vary, so stay updated with the Girona Tourist Office for upcoming events.

Flower Markets

Throughout the year, Girona blossoms with vibrant flower markets, transforming squares into colorful displays. While the renowned Temps de Flors (Flower Time) in May steals the spotlight, smaller flower markets also bloom seasonally, adding floral beauty to your visit.

Boutique Gems

While the markets offer a taste of local life, Girona's charming boutiques cater to diverse tastes and budgets. Here are a few unique shops to ignite your shopping spree:

Style Hub Despiral: Explore trendy and unique women's fashion at Carrer de Santa Clara, 43, where Despiral showcases a curated selection of clothing and accessories from independent designers with a touch of retro flair.

Espadrille Haven Toni Pons: Step into Toni Pons, an iconic destination since 1947, offering a vast selection of high-quality espadrilles at various locations. From classic to contemporary designs, find the perfect pair to elevate your summer style.

Treasure Trove Gluki: Discover unique finds at Plaça de la Independència, 3, where Gluki offers handcrafted ceramics, locally-made textiles, gourmet food products, and quirky homeware items, perfect for adding Catalan charm to your home.

Chocolate Paradise Chocolataria Equador Girona: Indulge in delectable chocolates at Santa Clara, 21, where Chocolataria Equador Girona crafts ethically sourced chocolates using traditional methods, offering a sweet souvenir for chocolate aficionados.

Stationery Oasis Papers: Unleash your creativity at Carrer Ballesteries, 20, where Papers presents a curated selection of exquisite notebooks, writing instruments, and unique paper goods, perfect for inspiring your creativity or adorning your desk.

Additional Tips

Market Exploration Hours: Markets typically operate from 8 am to 2 pm, while boutique hours vary from 10 am to 8 pm, with some shops closed during siesta time (1:30 pm to 5 pm).

Embrace Local Discoveries: Wander the charming backstreets to discover hidden boutiques and unique finds from local designers and artisans.

Tax-Free Shopping: Tourists spending over €90 in a single store may be eligible for a VAT refund; inquire at shops for details.

Enjoy Siesta: Use the midday break to enjoy a leisurely lunch or explore Girona's picturesque streets at your own pace.

EVENTS AND FESTIVALS

- Temps de Flors
- Girona Jazz Festival
- Sant Narcís Festival
- Cultural Events Throughout the Year

10. Events and Festivals

Temps de Flors

Girona Temps de Flors

Each spring, Girona celebrates the renowned Girona Temps de Flors, a nine-day festival that transforms the city with vibrant colors, flavors, and art. More than just a floral exhibition, it offers a unique way to explore Girona. By following the exhibition trail, you'll discover hidden nooks and crannies not found in guidebooks, including private patios and institutional buildings typically closed to the public. While much of the exhibition is concentrated in the old quarter, it also provides an opportunity to explore other parts of the city that visitors might usually overlook.

Girona Temps de Flors allows you to rediscover many parts of Girona. This year, the exhibition encourages exploration of the city's neighborhoods on foot or by bicycle, inviting you to admire the flowers, monuments, and natural beauty, and to be surprised by the city's landmarks, which take on a unique appearance during the festival.

From May 11th to 19th, the 69th edition of Girona Temps de Flors will feature 126 projects in 106 iconic spaces around the city. The festival began in 1954 during the Franco dictatorship, created by the Women's Section of the Falange as an exhibition of flowers and plants in the Rest Hall of the Municipal Theatre. A few years later, it relocated to the Romanesque monasteries of Sant Pere de Galligants and Sant Domènec. It wasn't until 1992 that it expanded to various parts of Girona's old town, as it is known today.

Girona Temps de Flors is a pure celebration of spring, with the entire city participating. Associations and organizations prepare each exhibition, shopkeepers decorate their windows, restaurants offer floral-themed menus, and concerts and events take place throughout the week.

Girona Jazz Festival

The Girona Jazz Festival has a storied history, celebrating the rich legacy of jazz while also embracing contemporary interpretations. Established in 1993, the festival has grown in stature and reputation, drawing internationally renowned artists as well as showcasing local talent. Over the years, it has become a key platform for both established and emerging musicians, fostering a deep appreciation for jazz in all its forms.

One of the festival's hallmarks is its eclectic lineup. From traditional jazz and bebop to avant-garde and fusion, the Girona Jazz Festival offers something for every jazz aficionado. Past editions have featured legendary performers such as Chick Corea, Brad Mehldau, and Esperanza Spalding, alongside innovative acts pushing the boundaries of the genre.

Girona's historic venues add a unique charm to the festival experience. Concerts are held in a variety of locations, from the grand Teatre Municipal and the contemporary Auditori de Girona to more intimate settings like the Plaça de la Independència and various cozy bars and clubs throughout the city. These venues, each with its own distinct atmosphere, allow for a diverse and immersive musical journey.

The festival is not just about performances; it also serves as an educational platform. Workshops and masterclasses are a significant component, offering budding musicians and enthusiasts the opportunity to learn from the masters. These sessions cover a wide range of topics, from instrumental techniques and improvisation to the history and evolution of jazz.

A sense of community and collaboration pervades the Girona Jazz Festival. Local musicians often share the stage with international stars, fostering a spirit of camaraderie and mutual respect. The festival also collaborates with various cultural institutions and educational establishments, further enriching Girona's cultural landscape.

The Girona Jazz Festival is a family-friendly event, with programs designed to engage younger audiences. Special concerts and interactive sessions introduce children to the world of jazz, ensuring that the love for this timeless genre is passed on to future generations.

No visit to Girona would be complete without indulging in its culinary delights. The festival period sees the city's restaurants and cafes buzzing with activity, offering special menus and jazz-themed evenings. From traditional Catalan dishes to innovative fusion cuisine, Girona's gastronomic scene provides the perfect accompaniment to the musical feast.

The Girona Jazz Festival typically takes place in October, with tickets available for individual concerts as well as festival passes for the entire event. It's advisable to book early, as popular performances tend to sell out quickly. Detailed schedules and ticketing information can be found on the festival's official website and at local tourist information centers.

Sant Narcís Festival

Sant Narcís Festival in Girona

Welcome to Girona, where tradition meets celebration during the vibrant Sant Narcís Festival! Held annually in honor of the city's patron saint, Sant Narcís, this festival transforms the streets into a lively spectacle of music, dance, gastronomy, and cultural events. Whether you're a local or a visitor, immerse yourself in the festive spirit and experience the essence of Girona's rich heritage.

When and Where

The Sant Narcís Festival typically takes place in late October, spanning over a week of festivities. The heart of the action unfolds in the historic center of Girona, with various events and activities scattered throughout the city streets, plazas, and venues.

Key Highlights

Opening Parade: Kick off the festivities with the grand parade, featuring colorful floats, traditional giants (gegants), and lively music winding through the city streets.

Concerts and Performances: Enjoy live music concerts showcasing a diverse range of genres, from traditional Catalan music to contemporary sounds, held in outdoor venues and concert halls across Girona.

Correfoc: Witness the exhilarating Correfoc, or "fire run," where costumed devils dance through the streets amidst fireworks and pyrotechnics, creating a mesmerizing spectacle.

Castellers: Marvel at the impressive human towers as teams compete to build the tallest and most intricate castells, a Catalan tradition symbolizing strength, unity, and teamwork.

Gastronomic Delights: Indulge in the culinary delights of Girona during the festival, with food stalls offering a tempting array of local specialties, including traditional Catalan dishes and festive treats.

Fireworks Display: Conclude each evening with a spectacular fireworks display lighting up the night sky, creating a magical ambiance over the city.

Traditional Games and Activities: Join in the fun with a variety of traditional games, workshops, and activities suitable for all ages, providing a glimpse into Catalan culture and heritage.

Practical Tips

Transportation: Plan your transportation within Girona accordingly, as certain streets may be closed for events or parades. Consider using public transportation or walking to navigate the city center.

Safety: Be mindful of large crowds during popular events and keep an eye on personal belongings. Follow any safety instructions provided during fireworks displays or other pyrotechnic events.

Language: While Catalan is the predominant language, many locals also speak Spanish and English. Learning a few basic Catalan phrases can enhance your festival experience and interaction with residents.

Weather: Check the weather forecast before attending outdoor events, and dress appropriately for the season, as temperatures in late October can vary.

Cultural Events Throughout the Year

Girona, a picturesque city nestled in the northeastern region of Catalonia, Spain, is not only renowned for its stunning architecture and rich history but also for its vibrant cultural scene. Throughout the year, Girona hosts a plethora of cultural events that cater to various interests, ranging from music and art to gastronomy and literature. Whether you're a history enthusiast, a foodie, or an art aficionado, there's something for everyone to enjoy in Girona. Here's a detailed guide to the cultural events you can experience throughout the year:

January - March

Temps de Flors (May Flower Festival): Taking place in May, this event transforms the city into a floral paradise. Streets, patios, and historic sites are adorned with colorful flower displays, creating a breathtaking spectacle. Visitors can wander through the narrow alleys of the Old Town, marveling at the creative floral arrangements while enjoying live music and traditional Catalan cuisine.

April - June

Girona, Temps de Cinema (Girona Film Festival): Film enthusiasts flock to Girona in June for this annual celebration of cinema. The festival showcases a diverse selection of films, including international releases, independent productions, and works by emerging filmmakers. In addition to film screenings, there are also workshops, panel discussions, and opportunities to meet industry professionals.

Girona a Capella (Girona A Cappella Festival): Music takes center stage during this festival, which highlights the beauty of a cappella singing. Choirs from around the world gather in Girona to perform a wide range of musical genres, from classical and sacred music to contemporary and pop. Concerts are held in various historic venues across the city, providing a unique backdrop for the performances.

July - September

Girona International Festival of Music (Girona Music Festival): Classical music aficionados won't want to miss this prestigious festival, held in July and August. Renowned musicians and orchestras from around the globe converge in Girona to perform masterpieces by classical composers in iconic venues such as the Cathedral and the Auditorium.

Girona Film Festival (GIFF): This film festival, held annually in September, celebrates the art of filmmaking with screenings of feature films, documentaries, and short films from both established and emerging filmmakers. In addition to film screenings, there are also workshops, panel discussions, and networking events for industry professionals and film enthusiasts alike.

October - December

Girona Jazz Festival: Jazz lovers rejoice during this annual festival, which showcases the best of contemporary jazz from local and international artists. Concerts are held in intimate venues throughout the city, providing an opportunity to experience the magic of live jazz in a unique setting.

Girona Gastronomy Festival: Foodies flock to Girona in November for this culinary extravaganza, which celebrates the region's rich gastronomic heritage. Local chefs showcase their culinary talents through cooking demonstrations, tastings, and special menus featuring traditional Catalan dishes with a modern twist.

Girona, Temps de Flors (Christmas Edition): The magic of Temps de Flors returns in December with a special Christmas edition. The city is decked out in festive decorations, and the streets come alive with holiday-themed flower displays, concerts, and activities for the whole family to enjoy.

NIGHTLIFE AND ENTERTAINMENT

- Bars and Pubs
- Nightclubs and Music Venues

11. Nightlife and Entertainment

Bars and Pubs

Assorted Bars for Any Time of Day in Girona

Looking for a place to enjoy a refreshing drink and a tasty snack at any time of the day? Girona boasts a variety of charming bars and cafes that cater to every palate and preference. Whether you're craving traditional tapas, a wide selection of beers, or stunning views of the city, there's something for everyone to enjoy. Here are some top picks for bars in Girona:

1. El Vermutet de Can Gombau

Location: Plaça de la Independència, 10

Experience the authentic atmosphere of a neighborhood social center at El Vermutet de Can Gombau. This cozy bar offers a delicious range of traditional tapas, including XXL olives, anchovies, and potato omelette, perfect for a pre-lunch snack. Enjoy a glass of vermouth or a small beer at great prices while soaking in the local ambiance. With its wooden tables and stools, this spot is ideal for spontaneous get-togethers and community camaraderie.

2. El Primer Glop

Indulge in the pleasure of the first sip at El Primer Glop, a haven for beer enthusiasts. Choose from a wide range of beers, including pale ales, red ales, and toasted varieties, from around a dozen taps and over 200 bottles. The knowledgeable staff can recommend the perfect brew to suit your taste preferences. Pair your beer with house tapas such as 'chistorra' (spicy sausage) and potato omelette for a true beer lover's paradise experience.

3. Cu-Cut

Location: Centre (Off Plaça de la Independència)

Since 1983, Cu-Cut has been a favorite among generations of locals for its laid-back atmosphere and diverse music selection. By day, it's a cozy café, and by night, it transforms into a lively bar tucked away off Plaça de la Independència. Enjoy a selection of pop, rock, and reggae music while sipping on house cocktails like mojitos and caipirinhas. Cu-Cut is the perfect spot for a casual drink and a dose of authentic Girona culture.

4. McKiernans

Location: Centre (Near La Rambla)

Transport yourself to Dublin without leaving Girona at McKiernans, an authentic Irish pub near La Rambla. Adorned with furniture made from wood sourced from Wexford Cathedral, this pub offers a wide range of beers, including Guinness and Duvel. Celebrate Saint Patrick's Day in style with green top hats and shamrocks as part of the festivities. McKiernans is your go-to destination for an Irish pub experience in the heart of Girona.

5. Cafè L'Arc

Location: Centre (Café bars)

With its unbeatable location overlooking the cathedral, Cafè L'Arc offers breathtaking views and a vibrant atmosphere. Popular among artists, students, and tourists alike, this café has been a Girona landmark for over 50 years. Savor a coffee made with fresh organic milk or indulge in a snowball cocktail while taking in the sights. Treat yourself to traditional Catalan dishes such as 'pa amb tomaquet' and patates braves for a truly satisfying culinary experience.

6. Lapsus Cafè

Location: Corner of Plaça de la Independència, near the Post Office

By day, Lapsus Cafè is a cozy spot for coffee and soft drinks, and by night, it transforms into a lively bar perfect for starting your evening with a gin and tonic, mixer, or beer. Its exceptional terrace makes it a memorable place to unwind, accompanied by ambient music during the day and livelier tunes at night.

7. El Sol

Location: Under the arches of Plaça del Vi

A traditional and unpretentious café, El Sol is ideally located with views of the City Hall balcony and the historical bookshop Les Voltes. Whether you're a tourist or a local, it's a great place for coffee, juice, soft drinks, or beer, and some light bites. The cobblestone terrace offers a unique vantage point for watching events in the square or simply taking a break from the bustling city.

8. A VBeure

For craft beer enthusiasts, A VBeure is a must-visit. They offer a wide range of beers from six different taps and over 50 bottled varieties, including local favorites like Moska and international selections like Belgian Orval. Pair your drinks with delicious 'pinxos' (tapas on small slices of bread) and specially crafted tapas to complement the beer flavors.

9. Llibreria-cafè Context

Location: Plaça del Pou Rodó

Combining a love for books, music, and good food, Llibreria-cafè Context is a cultural hub in Girona. Enjoy a coffee or glass of wine while attending a poetry recital or small concert. The café offers a selection of wines, beers, and liquors, along with plates of cured meats, cheeses, 'pinxos,' and salads. Its warm ambiance and friendly service, along with a magnificent terrace, make it an unmissable spot.

10. La Terra

Location: C/Ballesteries

A creative and charming café, La Terra is perfect for those looking to jot down ideas, draw, or simply relax. Overlooking the river Onyar, this bar offers a variety of drinks including teas, fresh juices, craft beers, and homemade hamburgers. The mosaic floors and unique décor add to its inviting atmosphere.

11. The River Café

Location: In front of 'the bottom of the lioness' sculpture and the basilica of Sant Fèlix

Open from 9am until the early hours, The River Café is a versatile spot for any time of the day. Enjoy their famous kebabs ('fletxes'), a menu suitable for celiacs, and a wide selection of over 60 beers and around 30 gins. With great music and a pet-friendly policy, it's an ideal place to relax and enjoy the local vibe.

Nightclubs and Music Venues

Nightlife and Live Music Venues in Girona

Girona offers a vibrant and diverse nightlife scene with bars, clubs, and live music venues catering to every taste. Whether you're looking to enjoy live jazz, dance to indie tunes, or savor cocktails in a chic setting, Girona has something for everyone. Here's a detailed guide to some of the best nightlife spots in the city:

1. Sunset Jazz Club

Address: Carrer d'En Jaume Pons Martí, 12, Girona, Spain

Contact: +34 872 08 01 45

Sunset Jazz Club, Girona's only jazz club and one of the city's greatest live music venues, provides a comfortable environment for listening, dancing, and chatting with friends. The club hosts various types of jazz, funk, soul, blues, folk, and even tango. With its intimate atmosphere and high-quality performances, it's a must-visit for music lovers.

2. Lola Cafè

Address: Carrer Bonaventura Carreras Peralta, 7, Girona, Spain

Contact: +34 972 22 88 24

Tucked away in Girona's old Jewish Quarter, Lola Cafè is the hub of the city's rumba scene. Its modern and baroque-style decor provides a unique backdrop for live performances and lively dancing. The café offers a fun environment with delicious cocktails and regular live music nights.

3. Sala la Mirona

Address: Carrer d'Amnistia Internacional, Girona, Spain

Contact: +34 972 23 23 75

As Girona's main venue for large-scale concerts, Sala la Mirona has hosted a wide range of acts, from local rock bands to DJ parties and tribute bands. This versatile space is perfect for enjoying live music and energetic performances in a larger setting.

4. One Girona

Address: Carrer Figuerola, 25, Girona, Spain

Contact: +34 972 48 56 00

Combining an urban nightclub and sushi bar, One Girona offers a stylish option for dining, dancing, and drinking. The industrial chic vibe, with exposed brick walls and metal pipes, sets the scene for inventive cocktails and delectable sushi plates. Guest and resident DJs play a mix of tunes to keep the dance floor lively.

5. Lux

Address: Carrer Figuerola, 50, Girona, Spain

Contact: +34 972 48 38 60

A favorite among the student crowd, Lux is a discotheque and pub known for its vibrant atmosphere and latest hits blasting from the sound system. Thursday nights are especially popular, making it the perfect time to experience what Lux has to offer.

6. Nou Platea

Address: Jeroni Reial de Fontclara, 2-6, Girona

Contact: +34 972 22 72 88

Located in the historic Albéniz Theatre, Nou Platea is one of Girona's most iconic nightspots. The large event space hosts concerts, workshops, social events, and shows. Thursday is student night with dance rhythms, Friday features a mix of Top 40 tunes, and Saturday is dedicated to deep house.

7. Yeah! Indie Club

Address: Avinguda de Ramon Folch, 9, Girona, Spain

Contact: +34 667 49 45 23

The go-to venue for indie music enthusiasts, Yeah! Indie Club offers a unique style with local bands, guest DJs, and special guest indie-rock bands. The club guarantees a great night out with excellent music and an energetic atmosphere.

12. Day Trips and Excursions

Figueres and the Dalí Museum

A Day Trip to Figueres and the Dalí Museum from Girona

Embark on a captivating journey into the world of Salvador Dalí with a day trip from Girona to Figueres, the birthplace of this artistic genius. Figueres, a charming town in Catalonia, Spain, not only offers a glimpse into Dalí's life and inspirations but also houses the world-renowned Dalí Theatre-Museum, a surreal masterpiece in itself.

Planning Your Day Trip

Distance and Transportation: Figueres is located approximately 40 kilometers northeast of Girona, with several convenient transportation options available:

Train: Enjoy the fastest and most comfortable journey with direct train service from Girona station to Figueres Vilafant station, taking about 25 minutes. Trains operate regularly throughout the day.

Bus: Opt for a more budget-friendly option with public buses, offering a travel time of about an hour. Buses depart from Girona bus station and arrive at Figueres bus station.

Car: For flexibility and the opportunity to explore at your own pace, consider renting a car. The drive takes 45 minutes to an hour, depending on traffic.

Guided Tours vs. Independent Travel: Choose between organized tours from Girona for a hassle-free experience including transportation, guided museum commentary, and sometimes lunch. Alternatively, plan your own trip using public transportation or a rented car. Audio guides are available for rent at the museum in multiple languages.

Exploring Figueres

Dalí Theatre-Museum: Delve into the crown jewel of Figueres, the Dalí Theatre-Museum, an absolute must-see. Designed by Dalí himself, the museum is a living testament to his surrealist vision. Explore a labyrinthine collection of his paintings, sculptures, installations, and even jewelry, all showcasing his unique artistic style. The iconic egg-topped exterior and the Rainy Cadillac installation in the courtyard are just the beginning of a truly surreal experience.

Figueres Toy Museum: Gain insight into Dalí's childhood and artistic influences at the Toy Museum (Museu del Joguet). This charming museum features a collection of antique toys and games, offering a glimpse into the world that may have sparked the artist's imagination.

Rambla de Figueres: Take a leisurely stroll down the lively Rambla, Figueres' main pedestrian street. Lined with shops, cafes, and restaurants, it's the perfect place to immerse yourself in the local atmosphere and enjoy a meal before or after your museum visit.

Additional Tips

Tickets & Opening Hours: Purchase tickets for the Dalí Theatre-Museum online in advance, especially during peak season, to avoid long queues. Opening hours vary by season, so check the museum's website for current information.

Dress Code: While there's no specific dress code for the museum, comfortable shoes are recommended as you'll be doing a fair amount of walking.

Combine with Other Activities: If time permits, explore the nearby medieval village of Peralada, renowned for its castle and summer music festival. Alternatively, venture to the Empordà wine region for a delightful wine tasting experience.

Besalú

The Medieval Bridge

Girona is not only ideal for day trips to Costa Brava but also to explore mountainous areas. One such destination easily accessible from Girona is Besalú, a small medieval town renowned for its impressive medieval bridge and rich historical heritage. Its narrow old-town streets house one of the best-preserved Jewish quarters in Europe.

Besalú is perfect for wandering, especially during the off-season or early in the morning. Photography enthusiasts will find it a must-visit spot, not only for the iconic bridge but for the entire historical complex, offering numerous photo opportunities. Additionally, HBO used Besalú's old town as a location for its TV series "Westworld."

One of the most beautiful and authentic medieval towns in Catalonia, Besalú's unique vibe is comparable to only a few other villages in the region, such as Castellfollit de la Roca. The village has preserved its charm, and crossing the medieval bridge feels like stepping back in time, with its narrow cobblestone streets, charming houses, and historical buildings.

Where is Besalú Located?

Besalú is situated in Garrotxa county, known for its volcanic formations and mountains. Its size and location make it ideal for a tranquil one-day trip from Girona, as it is less than 40 km from the provincial capital. Barcelona is also within a reasonable driving distance (140 km), but staying in Girona or finding accommodation in Besalú or nearby towns like Olot is recommended.

Besalú is a popular tourist destination, especially during the summer. To avoid the crowds, plan your visit in advance and aim to visit outside the peak hours of 11 am to 6 pm.

How to Get to Besalú

The best way to reach Besalú is by car. Renting a car is a good idea if you plan to explore northern Catalonia, including the Pyrenees and Costa Brava, both ideal for road trips. Parking in Besalú is convenient, with several free parking areas at the village entrance. While public transport options exist, traveling between villages or cities can be tedious. Other ways to reach Besalú include biking or taking a taxi, though the latter can be expensive.

Things to See and Do in Besalú

Besalú, a picturesque medieval town in Catalonia, has gained popularity due to its Instagram-worthy bridge, historical charm, and appearances in TV series like HBO's "Westworld." Here are the top attractions and activities to enjoy in Besalú:

1. Besalú Bridge (El Pont de Besalú)

The most iconic landmark of Besalú, this Romanesque bridge dates back to the 11th century. The bridge, with its 8 arches (7 visible) and an imposing tower, has been reconstructed multiple times due to flooding. For a unique perspective, take the stairs on the left-hand side when coming from the parking area to view the bridge and old town from the riverside.

2. Bridge Viewpoints

There are two notable viewpoints in the old town for different views of the bridge:

The first offers a classic view of the bridge, tower, and arches.

The second provides a more elevated and parallel perspective of the bridge.

3. Jewish Bathhouse & Jewish Quarter

Explore one of the most well-preserved medieval Jewish quarters in Spain. The Jewish Bathhouse (Mikveh), hidden within the Jewish Quarter's winding streets, is one of the four such bathhouses in Europe. Visits are guided by the local Tourism Office. The Jewish Quarter is also home to La Plaça de la Llibertat, a filming location for HBO's "Westworld."

4. Sant Pere de Besalú

This 10th-century monastery, built in a Romanesque style, is part of Besalú's historical heritage. It's notable for its simplicity and lack of detailed decoration compared to other cathedrals. Visits must be booked through the tourism office.

5. Circusland

A unique museum dedicated to the art of the circus, Circusland offers a comprehensive history of circus arts and houses the world's largest miniature circus. It's a great spot for circus enthusiasts and families with children.

6. Old Town and Churches

Wander the narrow cobblestone streets of Besalú's old town, filled with charming houses, churches, and hidden details. Look for the various chair sculptures scattered throughout the town, created by local artists.

Top Photography Locations in Besalú

The Bridge: The most iconic element, perfect for capturing the essence of Besalú.

Old Town: Full of hidden gems and picturesque details.

Viewpoints: Offering different angles of the bridge and the city.

Riverside: Ideal for capturing the old town with reflections in the river.

Churches: Including Sant Pere de Besalú and other lesser-known churches.

Banyoles and Its Lake

The Perfect Lake

This small city, with its charming village atmosphere, boasts one of the most beautiful lakes in the region. Whether it's the quaint fisherman's huts or the stunning sunset views, Banyoles is worth a visit. Located just a 30-minute drive from Girona, it feels like an entirely different world. Even if you don't have a car, there are plenty of buses and other transportation options available to reach Banyoles.

How to Get to Banyoles

Banyoles is the capital of the Pla de l'Estany county, one of the smallest counties in Catalonia. It is situated 25 km (15 miles) north of Girona, the provincial capital and one of Catalonia's most beautiful cities. Many visitors stay in Girona and use it as a base to explore nearby attractions like Banyoles.

Reaching Banyoles from Girona is very straightforward, and you won't need to take toll roads. There are multiple entrances to the city, but all lead to the lake. Since you'll likely spend time walking around the lake, it doesn't matter which entrance you use or where you park.

The Lake: Activities

Hiking

One of the most popular activities in Banyoles is hiking. A well-marked circuit around the lake spans about 6 km and takes less than 1.5 hours to complete. Take your time to explore the distinctive fisherman huts, footbridges, spot wildlife (mainly birds), and enjoy the scenic views. For a more challenging hike, consider trekking up Puig Clarà for a panoramic view of the area and the lake. This hike begins at Porqueres, a little community on the lake, and there are numerous trails and signs to direct you. You can even combine this hike with the lake circuit. Don't hesitate to ask locals for directions, but note that they might not speak English.

Banyoles revolves around its lake. Visiting on a Saturday or Sunday morning, you'll see a variety of people walking, running, or cycling around the lake, showcasing the strong connection between the city and the water. Rowing and swimming are also common activities. Fun fact: Banyoles hosted the rowing competitions for the 1992 Barcelona Olympic Games!

Swimming

In the summer, swimming is allowed in designated areas of the lake. Although the water is not crystal-clear due to a silty bottom, these areas ensure safe swimming. Some swimming spots charge a fee, but there is a free area where you can swim and enjoy the sunset from the water. If you're into competitive swimming, Banyoles hosts several competitions throughout the year, including the famous lake crossing, which has even featured Olympic swimmers like Mireia Belmonte.

Renting a Boat

A classic activity in Banyoles is renting one of the small white and blue rowing boats. It's a tourist favorite, providing a beautiful way to explore the lake from a different perspective. Prices vary by season. If boating isn't your preference, there are plenty of other activities around the lake.

La Draga

Add a cultural and historical dimension to your visit by exploring the Neolithic Settlement of La Draga. This site is one of the earliest lakeside Neolithic settlements discovered in Europe. The humid environment has preserved many tools and artifacts, and the site now functions as an open-air museum with reconstructed huts, fields, and daily life scenes. Nearby, the Park de la

Draga offers a large space ideal for picnics and children's play.

Photography

Banyoles is a photographer's paradise, offering a blend of nature, landscape, and wildlife photography. Early mornings are perfect for spotting animals, mainly birds, around the lake. Sunrises and sunsets provide stunning photographic opportunities. Some favorite photography spots include:

Sunrise: Best viewed from the wilder, less inhabited end of the lake. Look for windless days to capture reflections on the water, using footbridges as foreground elements.

Sunset: Best admired from the bathing area or near the floating fisherman huts, which make excellent main elements for photos.

Boats: The white and blue rowing boats are ideal subjects for sunset photos. Experiment with long exposures on slightly windy days for interesting effects.

Athletes: The lake is a hub of activity, with cyclists, rowers, swimmers, and runners providing dynamic subjects for action shots.

Reflections & Fisherman Huts: On calm, windless days, reflections are abundant. Aim for the fisherman huts, iconic elements of the lake's scenery.

Montserrat Mountain

A Day Trip to Montserrat Mountain from Girona

Towering over the Catalonian landscape, Montserrat Mountain offers a captivating blend of spirituality, breathtaking scenery, and cultural heritage. A day trip from Girona to Montserrat is a perfect way to escape the city bustle and experience the serenity of the mountain sanctuary, famed for its Benedictine monastery and the Black Madonna statue.

Planning Your Ascent

Distance and Transportation: Montserrat Monastery is approximately 60 kilometers northwest of Girona. Convenient transportation options include:

Organized Tour: Join a guided tour from Girona, which typically includes transportation, skip-the-line tickets for the monastery, and insightful commentary from a knowledgeable guide.

Train & Cable Car: Take the RENFE train from Girona station to Montserrat-Vila station. Then, ascend the mountainside to the monastery via a funicular railway or cable car. Check timetables and combined tickets for train and funicular/cable car.

Car & Rack Railway: Drive to Montserrat Monastery car park (parking fees apply) and take the cremallera (rack railway) for the final leg of the journey.

Time of Year: Montserrat is a year-round destination, but weather conditions vary. Spring and autumn offer pleasant temperatures, while summers can be hot and crowded. Winter may bring cold and occasional snow, so dress accordingly.

Exploring Montserrat

Montserrat Monastery: Explore the Benedictine monastery, the spiritual heart of the mountain. Marvel at the majestic basilica housing the revered Black Madonna statue, a dark wood carving of the Virgin Mary. Discover the cloisters, museums, and other public areas (admission fees may apply).

Scenic Views: Enjoy breathtaking panoramic views of the Catalonian countryside. Take a funicular or cable car ride for stunning aerial vistas, or hike along trails for breathtaking panoramas and a connection with nature.

Montserrat Boys' Choir: Experience the angelic voices of the Escolania de Montserrat, a boys' choir with a centuries-old tradition of singing religious music in the basilica. Check the schedule for performance times (additional ticket might be required).

Audiovisual Exhibition: Delve into Montserrat's history and significance with the audiovisual exhibition (additional ticket might be required). Learn about the monastery's role in Catalan culture and the spiritual significance of the Black Madonna.

Sampling Local Products: Try delicious local products made by the monks, such as honey, cheese, and liqueurs, available for purchase at monastery shops.

Additional Tips

Dress Code: Respectful attire is recommended as the monastery is a place of worship.

Comfortable Shoes: Be prepared for walking on uneven terrain, especially if exploring hiking trails.

Food Options: Several restaurants and cafes near the monastery offer a variety of food. Alternatively, pack a picnic lunch to enjoy with stunning views.

PRACTICAL INFORMATION

- Emergency Contacts
- Health and Safety
- Local Customs and Etiquette
- Basic Catalan Phrases

13. Practical Information

Emergency Contacts

Emergency Numbers

Emergency Services (General): Dial 112 for immediate assistance in case of emergencies requiring police, fire, or medical assistance. This number is toll-free and operates 24/7, ensuring prompt response to any emergency situation.

Medical Emergencies: For urgent medical attention or ambulance services, dial 061. Trained medical professionals will respond promptly to assess and address your medical needs, providing necessary care and transportation to the nearest healthcare facility.

Police Assistance: Contact the Mossos d'Esquadra, Catalonia's police force, by dialing 088 in case of non-emergency situations requiring police intervention, such as reporting a crime or seeking assistance with safety concerns.

Fire and Rescue Services: For emergencies related to fires, accidents, or other incidents requiring fire and rescue services, dial 080. Highly trained firefighters will respond promptly to mitigate risks and provide assistance as needed.

Additional Contacts

Girona Tourist Information: If you require assistance or information regarding local services, attractions, or accommodations, contact the Girona Tourist Information Office at +34 972 226 575 or visit their office located at Plaça de Catalunya, 17.

Consular Services: In the event of emergencies involving foreign nationals, such as lost passports or legal issues, contact your country's consulate or embassy for assistance. Consular contact information can typically be found on official government websites or through directory assistance services.

Practical Tips

Be Prepared: Keep important emergency numbers stored in your phone contacts and readily accessible in case of emergencies.

Stay Calm: In emergency situations, remain calm and provide clear and concise information when contacting emergency services to ensure swift and effective response.

Know Your Location: Be aware of your surroundings and provide accurate details about your location when contacting emergency services to facilitate their response.

Seek Assistance: Don't hesitate to seek assistance from locals, hotel staff, or authorities if you encounter any emergency situation or require help navigating unfamiliar circumstances.

Health and Safety

Health Precautions

When visiting Girona, it's essential to prioritize your health. Begin by ensuring you have comprehensive travel insurance that covers medical expenses and emergency evacuation if needed. Additionally, check with your healthcare provider or a travel health clinic to determine if any vaccinations are recommended for your trip. If you take prescription medications, ensure you have an adequate supply for the duration of your stay and carry them in their original packaging along with a copy of your prescription. Girona enjoys plenty of sunshine, so protect yourself from sunburn by wearing sunscreen, a hat, and sunglasses, especially during peak sun hours. Lastly, stay hydrated by carrying a refillable water bottle and drinking plenty of fluids throughout the day.

Safety Tips

While exploring Girona, it's crucial to stay vigilant and aware of your surroundings. Be cautious in crowded tourist areas to avoid potential scams, pickpocketing, or other petty crimes. Keep your belongings secure at all times, especially in crowded places, by using a money belt, anti-theft bag, or hotel safe. Familiarize yourself with emergency phone numbers for local police, medical services, and your country's embassy or consulate. Exercise caution when navigating the city at night, sticking to well-lit streets and traveling in groups, especially late at night. When crossing streets, obey traffic signals and look both ways, even on one-way streets.

Medical Assistance

Girona boasts modern medical facilities, including hospitals, clinics, and pharmacies, providing a range of healthcare services to residents and visitors alike. In case of medical emergencies, dial 112 for immediate assistance or 061 for medical emergencies specifically. Trained medical professionals will respond promptly to assess and address your medical needs. Pharmacies are readily available throughout Girona, offering over-the-counter medications, prescription drugs, and medical advice.

Food and Water Safety

Enjoy the culinary delights of Girona with confidence by patronizing reputable restaurants and eateries that adhere to high standards of food hygiene and safety. While tap water in Girona is generally safe for drinking, some visitors may prefer bottled water for peace of mind. Verify with your accommodation provider or restaurant if tap water is potable in specific locations.

Local Customs and Etiquette

Social Life and Etiquette

One of the most essential components of life in Girona is family; no celebration is complete without a large gathering, albeit this is more frequent outside of the big cities where modern life takes its toll. Nonetheless, the elderly are respected, and it is not uncommon to have older relatives being cared for in the family home. Similarly, children are completely embraced and included into everything.

Food is an important component of family life in Girona, with lunch (la comida) being the main meal of the day, often lasting from 2 to 4 p.m. It is normal for shops and entire villages to come to a halt for the afternoon meal and siesta, particularly in more remote locations. Evening dinners, which can begin as late as 10 p.m., are typically preceded by a leisurely stroll, or paseo, during which you can enjoy an aperitif at one or more bars.

Friends are more likely to meet for meals in restaurants, but if you are invited to someone's home for dinner, bring a small gift for any children, as well as chocolates, a bottle of wine, or some flowers (but avoid dahlias, chrysanthemums, and flowers in odd numbers, which are only given at funerals). Keep in mind that excessive drinking is uncommon, and while there appear to be bars on every corner, they are more for coffee and chatting than heavy drinking.

Girona has one of the highest rates of smoking in Europe, with an estimated 30% of the population smoking on a regular basis. However, attitudes are changing, and the legislation now prohibits smoking in all public areas, including shops, public transportation, pubs, and restaurants.

Tipping is widespread in Girona, but not always expected. Locals are minimal tippers; twenty cents on a bar table or five percent in a restaurant is usually adequate. It is also customary to tip taxi drivers, hotel porters, and other service personnel with little change.

If you intend to engage in any topless sunbathing, consider local feelings first, and attempt to stick to beaches where others are already doing so. If you enter a church, make sure you are appropriately covered; shorts and sleeveless tops are not permitted.

Greetings

If you meet someone for the first time in Girona, shake their hand. If you become friends, you may eventually progress to hugging (men) or kissing each cheek (women), beginning with the left. Men are also more likely to kiss women hello and goodbye than to shake their hands. To greet someone, use Buenos días before lunch and Buenas tardes after that. Remember that in Girona, the sense of time is somewhat elastic, so unless you're meeting for business (when being late is really bad form), don't be irritated if you're kept waiting for ten or twenty minutes.

Basic Catalan Phrases

To help you navigate interactions in Girona, here are some basic Catalan phrases:

Hello: Hola

Good morning: Bon dia

Good afternoon/evening: Bona tarda

Good night: Bona nit

Please: Si us plau

Thank you: Gràcies

You're welcome: De res

Excuse me: Perdó

Yes: Sí

No: No

Do you speak English?: Parles anglès?

How much does it cost?: Quant costa?

Using these phrases will endear you to the locals and can make everyday interactions smoother.

Pronunciation Tips

Catalan pronunciation can be challenging for newcomers. Here are some tips:

"C" before "e" or "i" sounds like an English "s."

"G" before "e" or "i" sounds like the English "j."

"Ny" is pronounced like the "ny" in "canyon."

The letter "l" at the end of words is often silent.

Practicing these sounds will help you communicate more effectively and understand spoken Catalan better.

Language in Public Places

Public signage in Girona is primarily in Catalan, with Spanish often included. Menus, tourist information, and public transportation signs are usually bilingual, ensuring accessibility for visitors. If you need help understanding a sign or menu, don't hesitate to ask for clarification in Spanish or English.

Learning Catalan

While fluency in Catalan is not necessary to enjoy your visit to Girona, learning a few key phrases shows cultural respect and can lead to more meaningful interactions. Language apps, phrasebooks, and online courses can help you familiarize yourself with basic Catalan before your trip.

Respecting the Local Culture

Catalans take great pride in their language and cultural identity. When addressing someone, starting with Catalan is always a good idea. If they respond in Spanish or English, you can switch accordingly. This practice demonstrates cultural sensitivity and enhances your connection with the locals.

Helpful Resources

For those interested in delving deeper into the language, Girona offers several resources:

Language exchange programs and meet-ups provide practice with native speakers.

Local bookstores carry bilingual books and language guides.

Many cafes and community centers offer language courses or informal conversation groups.

Taking advantage of these resources can deepen your understanding of Catalan and enrich your stay in Girona.

SUGGESTED ITINERARIES

- One-Day in Girona
- Three-Day Itinerary
- Week-Long Exploration

14. Suggested Itineraries

One-Day in Girona

Morning

8:30 AM - Breakfast at La Fabrica

Start your day with a delicious breakfast at La Fabrica, a popular café known for its specialty coffee and hearty breakfast options. Try their avocado toast or a classic croissant with freshly brewed coffee.

9:30 AM - Explore the Old Town (Barri Vell)

Head to the historic heart of Girona, the Old Town. Wander through the small, cobblestone streets, admiring the well-preserved medieval architecture.

Cathedral of Girona: Marvel at the impressive Gothic facade and climb the steps to enjoy panoramic views of the city. Inside, don't miss the Tapestry of Creation and the stunning nave, the widest Gothic nave in the world.

Basilica of Sant Feliu: Visit this beautiful basilica with its mix of Romanesque and Gothic architecture, and see the impressive tombs and sculptures.

11:00 AM - Walk Along the Onyar River

Stroll along the Onyar River and take in the colorful facades of the houses lining its banks. The best views can be enjoyed from one of the many bridges, particularly the Eiffel Bridge (Pont de les Peixateries Velles), designed by Gustave Eiffel before he built the Eiffel Tower.

11:30 AM - Visit the Jewish Quarter (El Call)

Explore El Call, one of Europe's most well-preserved Jewish districts. Wander through the labyrinthine streets and visit the Museum of Jewish History to learn about the rich history and heritage of Girona's Jewish community.

Afternoon

12:30 PM - Lunch at Llevataps

Enjoy a leisurely lunch at Llevataps, a highly regarded restaurant in the Old Town. Savor Catalan cuisine with dishes like grilled meats, seafood, and local specialties.

2:00 PM - Walk the Medieval Walls (Passeig de la Muralla)

After lunch, take a walk along the ancient city walls for stunning views of Girona and the surrounding countryside. The well-preserved walls date back to Roman times and offer several vantage points for great photo opportunities.

3:00 PM - Visit the Arab Baths (Banys Àrabs)

Explore the Arab Baths, a 12th-century Romanesque structure inspired by medieval Muslim baths. The site includes a frigidarium (cold room), tepidarium (warm room), and caldarium (hot room), and is a peaceful spot to reflect on the city's layered history.

3:30 PM - Relax in Plaça de la Independència

Take a break in Plaça de la Independència, one of Girona's most iconic squares. Enjoy a coffee or gelato at one of the many cafés surrounding the square and watch the world go by.

Evening

4:30 PM - Visit the Cinema Museum (Museu del Cinema)

Delve into the world of film and photography at the Cinema Museum. The museum offers fascinating exhibits on the history of cinema, including antique cameras, projectors, and film posters.

6:00 PM - Shopping in the Rambla de la Llibertat

Stroll along the Rambla de la Llibertat, a lively promenade lined with shops, boutiques, and market stalls. Pick up some souvenirs, local crafts, or gourmet treats to take home.

7:00 PM - Dinner at Cal Ros

Finish your day with a memorable dinner at Cal Ros, a restaurant known for its traditional Catalan dishes and cozy ambiance. Try the local specialties like botifarra (Catalan sausage) or suquet de peix (fish stew).

9:00 PM - Evening Stroll and Drinks

After dinner, take an evening stroll through the illuminated streets of the Old Town. For a nightcap, head to a bar like La Terra, where you can enjoy a glass of Catalan wine or a cocktail.

10:30 PM - Return to Your Accommodation

After a full day of exploring Girona, head back to your accommodation to rest and reflect on your memorable day in this enchanting city.

Three-Day Itinerary

Day 1: A Walk-Through Time

Morning: Exploring Medieval Marvels

Begin your day with a journey back in time. Start by visiting the imposing Girona Cathedral, marveling at its Gothic architecture and the breathtaking views from the rooftop (optional ticket). The cathedral's vast interior, featuring the widest Gothic nave in the world, is a sight to behold. Continue your historical walk by wandering the charming streets of the Old Town. Get lost in the maze of narrow alleyways and discover hidden squares. Don't miss the Arab Baths, a testament to Girona's multicultural past, with its well-preserved medieval bathhouse architecture.

Afternoon: Jewish Quarter Discovery

Head to the Jewish Quarter (El Call), one of the best-preserved Jewish quarters in Europe. Explore the labyrinthine streets, synagogues, and the Call Museum, learning about Girona's rich Jewish heritage. The museum provides a fascinating glimpse into the daily life and traditions of the Jewish community that once thrived here. In the afternoon, treat yourself to a delicious lunch at a traditional Catalan restaurant, savoring local flavors such as botifarra (Catalan sausage) and pa amb tomàquet (bread with tomato).

Evening: Riverfront Stroll and Flamenco Performance

As the sun sets, stroll along the Onyar River, taking in the vibrant colors of the houses lining the banks. The picturesque views are perfect for photos. Cap off the day with a flamenco performance, a captivating display of Spanish dance and music (optional ticket). The passionate rhythms and dramatic moves of flamenco will leave you mesmerized.

Day 2: Unveiling Artistic Gems & Culinary Delights

Morning: Artistic Exploration

Start your day at the Girona Art Museum, exploring a collection of Catalan art from the medieval period to the 20th century. The museum's exhibits range from Romanesque and Gothic to Renaissance and Baroque masterpieces. Next, delve into the world of Surrealism with a visit to the Cinema Museum, housed in a former cinema and showcasing a fascinating collection of movie memorabilia and interactive exhibits. This museum offers a unique perspective on the evolution of film and photography.

Afternoon: Market Visit and Cooking Class

Immerse yourself in the vibrant atmosphere of the Mercat del Lleó (Lion Market), a feast for the senses overflowing with fresh, local produce, cured meats, and artisan cheeses. Sample local delicacies and stock up on delicious souvenirs. In the afternoon, take a leisurely cooking class and learn the secrets of traditional Catalan cuisine. End your day by putting your newfound skills to the test, preparing a delicious dinner at the cooking school. This hands-on experience will give you a deeper appreciation for Catalan culinary traditions.

Evening: Leisurely Stroll and Local Nightlife

Enjoy a relaxing evening stroll through the charming streets of the Old Town, soaking up the city's unique atmosphere. For a touch of local nightlife, head to a bar or café in the Plaça de la Independència and people-watch as you sip on a refreshing drink. The lively square is a popular gathering spot for locals and visitors alike.

Day 3: Exploring Beyond the City Walls

Morning: Day Trip to Figueres or Pals

Dedicate your final day to exploring the captivating surroundings of Girona. Consider a day trip to Figueres, the birthplace of Salvador Dalí, and delve into the world of Surrealism at the renowned Dalí Theatre-Museum. The museum, designed by Dalí himself, is an immersive experience showcasing his eccentric works. Alternatively, explore the medieval village of Pals, perched on a hilltop and offering panoramic views of the surrounding countryside. Wander its cobblestone streets, admire its ancient stone houses, and soak in the historic ambiance.

Afternoon: Nature and Relaxation at Banyoles Lake

For a touch of nature, head to the nearby Banyoles Lake, the largest natural lake in Catalonia. Enjoy a boat ride on the lake, rent a bike and explore the surrounding trails, or simply relax by the water's edge. The tranquil setting is perfect for unwinding and reflecting on your Girona adventure.

Evening: Farewell Dinner and Night Stroll

Return to Girona for a final evening of exploration. Enjoy a farewell dinner at a restaurant with a rooftop terrace, savoring delicious food and the breathtaking views of the city. Restaurants like Mimolet and Divinum offer excellent dining experiences with scenic vistas. As the night unfolds, wander through the illuminated streets, bidding farewell to this captivating city. The beautifully lit monuments and quiet, serene streets create a magical ambiance for your last evening in Girona.

Week-Long Exploration

Girona, a captivating city in Catalonia, Spain, offers a treasure trove of experiences beyond a typical weekend getaway. With a week at your disposal, you can delve deeper into its rich history, vibrant culture, and artistic heritage while also venturing into the surrounding countryside for a taste of nature and charming villages. Here's a comprehensive guide to plan your perfect week-long exploration of Girona:

Day 1 & 2: Unveiling the City's Heart

Immerse Yourself in History

Dedicate the first two days to exploring Girona's historical core. Start with the imposing Girona Cathedral, marveling at its Gothic architecture and the breathtaking views from the rooftop (optional ticket). Wander through the charming streets of the Old Town, getting lost in the maze of narrow alleyways and discovering hidden squares. Don't miss the Arab Baths, a testament to Girona's multicultural past.

Jewish Quarter & Museum

Explore the Jewish Quarter (El Call), one of the best-preserved Jewish quarters in Europe. Delve into the labyrinthine streets, synagogues, and the Call Museum, learning about Girona's rich Jewish heritage.

Art and Cinema

Head to the Girona Art Museum, showcasing a collection of Catalan art from the medieval period to the 20th century. Next, delve into the world of Surrealism with a visit to the Cinema Museum, housed in a former cinema and offering fascinating movie memorabilia and interactive exhibits.

Day 3: A Culinary Adventure

Market Delights

Immerse yourself in the vibrant atmosphere of the Mercat del Lleó (Lion Market), a feast for the senses overflowing with fresh, local produce, cured meats, and artisan cheeses. Sample local delicacies and stock up on delicious souvenirs. In the afternoon, take a leisurely cooking class and learn the secrets of traditional Catalan cuisine. End your day by putting your newfound skills to the test, preparing a delicious dinner at the cooking school.

Food & Wine Pairing

For an extra treat, participate in a food and wine pairing experience, learning about the unique flavors of the region and how they complement each other. Indulge in a selection of local wines paired with delicious tapas or a multi-course meal.

Day 4: Medieval Marvels and Beyond

Figueres & Dalí

Dedicate a day to exploring the nearby town of Figueres, the birthplace of Salvador Dalí. Delve into the world of Surrealism at the renowned Dalí Theatre-Museum, a masterpiece in itself designed by the artist. Explore the town's charming streets and museums, or visit the Toy Museum for a glimpse into Dalí's childhood inspirations.

Medieval Escapade

Take a day trip to a quaint medieval village like Pals, which sits on a hilltop and provides panoramic views of the surrounding countryside. Explore its narrow streets, fortified walls, and historical landmarks.

Day 5: Nature's Embrace

Banyoles Lake

Escape the city bustle and head to the Banyoles Lake, the largest natural lake in Catalonia. Enjoy a boat ride on the lake, rent a bike and explore the surrounding trails, or simply relax by the water's edge and soak up the natural beauty. For the adventurous, explore the surrounding natural parks like La Garrotxa Volcanic Zone or the Les Gavarres Massif, offering hiking trails and stunning scenery.

Day 6: Local Festivals & Hidden Gems

Festival Fun

Check the local event calendar for any festivals or cultural events happening during your stay. Immerse yourself in the festive atmosphere, witness traditional performances, and experience the city's vibrant spirit.

Hidden Gems

Dedicate a day to exploring Girona's hidden corners. Wander off the beaten path, discover charming parks and gardens, or visit lesser-known museums like the History Museum of Girona or the Museum of Jewish History.

Shopping Spree

Unleash your inner shopaholic with a day dedicated to exploring Girona's vibrant shopping scene. From bustling markets like the weekly Art Fair or the Artisan Food Products Fair to charming boutiques showcasing local designers and handcrafted goods, there's something for everyone. In the evening, unwind at a traditional bar or café, enjoying tapas and drinks with the locals.

Day 7: Farewell & Final Touches

Relaxing Morning

Enjoy a leisurely breakfast at a café, people-watching and soaking up the city's atmosphere. Do some last-minute souvenir shopping or revisit a place that captured your heart during your exploration.

Farewell Dinner

Cap off your week-long adventure with a farewell dinner at a restaurant with a stunning view, savoring the delicious food and reminiscing about your memorable experiences in Girona. Consider dining at a rooftop restaurant to enjoy the breathtaking panorama of the city as you bid farewell.

Printed in Great Britain
by Amazon